FIGHTING FOR THE FRENCH
FOREIGN LEGION

FIGHTING FOR THE FRENCH

FOREIGN LEGION

ALEX LOCHRIE

Pen & Sword
MILITARY

First published in Great Britain in 2009
and reprinted in 2010 and 2011
Reprinted in this format in 2013, 2016 and 2017 by
PEN AND SWORD MILITARY
An imprint of
Pen & Sword Books Limited
47 Church Street
Barnsley
South Yorkshire
S70 2AS

ISBN 978 1 78337 615 5

A CIP catalogue record for this book is available from the British Library

Printed and bound in the UK
By CPI Group (UK) Ltd, Croydon, CR0 4YY

Pen & Sword Books Limited incorporates the imprints of Atlas,
Archaeology, Aviation, Discovery, Family History, Fiction, History, Maritime,
Military, Military Classics, Politics, Select, Transport, True Crime, Air World,
Frontline Publishing, Leo Cooper, Remember When, Seaforth Publishing,
The Praetorian Press, Wharncliffe Local History, Wharncliffe Transport,
Wharncliffe True Crime and White Owl.

For a complete list of Pen & Sword titles please contact
PEN & SWORD BOOKS LIMITED
47 Church Street, Barnsley, South Yorkshire S70 2AS, United Kingdom
E-mail: enquiries@pen-and-sword.co.uk
Website: www.pen-and-sword.co.uk

Contents

Acknowledgements

I would like to thank all those who have helped me get my story into print: my wife who encouraged me to write it; James Baillieu, who put me in touch with Henry Wilson of Pen & Sword Books; Bobby Gainher, my editor; and of course all the officers and legionnaires who accompanied me on my journey, who this book is really all about.

CHAPTER 1

Survivors

Life in the French Foreign Legion can be described in one word – tough! – particularly if you happen to be part of the elite world that is the 2ème Regiment Etranger de Parachutiste (2ème REP).

At the beginning of January 1985, my company was on the move again. The 1st Company specialized in commando warfare and, like everything else in the Legion, that meant some serious training. The expression 'No pain, no gain', must have originated in the Legion. We headed off to mainland France for a training course at France's number one commando training centre, Le Centre National d'Entrainement Commando (CNEC).

Our first week was spent at the town of Collioure, on the Mediterranean coast near the frontier with Spain. It is a town that has been the subject of many paintings, with its imposing fort perched on the cliffs overlooking the port. The French Army uses the old fort as a confidence-building centre before trainees progress on to the real thing at the commando training centre high in the Pyrenees, at Mont Louis. There were walls to climb, moats to cross and jumps from high to low walls with a 120-foot drop on the other side to the waves crashing onto the rocks below. There were roofs to clamber over and windows to abseil into. At the beginning of the week everyone was nervous, attacking the obstacles with caution and at walking pace. Security harnesses were worn at all times and anyone taking unnecessary risks was punished. Men thought to be acting recklessly found themselves off the course and working in the kitchens. Obstacles which seemed to be high and dangerous at the beginning of the week were now being taken at the double against the clock, which was exactly what was meant to happen. But this had just been a foretaste of what was in store for us before we moved up to the No.1 Commando Training Centre at Mont Louis – the real McCoy.

The drive up through the Pyrenees was breathtaking as we passed through some of the most beautiful countryside in Europe. After the relatively mild climate of Corsica and the Mediterranean coast, we quickly found ourselves at 2,000 metres above sea level and well above the snow line. Mont Louis is the highest town in France, the ancient fort dates back to the 1600s and was very impressive. All of this was set against a background of intimidating, snow-covered mountains, forests, lakes and it was very, very cold indeed. A brass monkey wouldn't have lasted five minutes.

The obstacle courses were graded into three degrees of difficulty and coded yellow, red and black. The CNEC does not expect everyone who comes here to attain the highest level, but the Legion does, and in particular the REP expects nothing less. Anyone failing to reach the highest level has no place in a commando company and would be moved to other duties within the Regiment on their return. Those who had to drop out through injury would get another chance to complete the course at a later date.

The facility is also used by foreign forces including the UK's Royal Marines, the SAS and the American Seals, and is acknowledged as being one of the best of its kind in the world. France has two other 'extreme warfare schools': the jungle warfare school in French Guyana and a commando training centre in Djibouti, both run by the Legion.

Physically, this was the hardest thing I have ever done. As at Collioure, instruction started at a walking pace, slowly building our skills and confidence to tackle the most dangerous parts of the course, the 'piste noir'. Again it was all about teamwork and having total confidence in those around you – this was not a game and mistakes could easily cost a life or lead to serious injury. Apart from the pure difficulty of the obstacles, the cold was playing a major part by covering everything in a thick coating of ice. The centre normally closed during the winter months but the Legion is the Legion and here we were. Gloves were normally optional, but without them your skin would have stuck to the cables. Once you accepted that the obstacles were passable and that many had done it before you, it became a question of self-confidence.

As the weeks passed, we became more gung-ho in our approach and the stopwatches began to come out. This was very physical for me and a real test to see if I could keep up with the youngsters, but there was more than the physical side to being a front-line commando. You can be one of the strongest men in the world but if you don't have the mental aptitude to attack the problems you are faced with, you won't get anywhere. Stamina also comes into the equation and that was where my age was a definite advantage. As ever, I was finding the obstacles hard going where arm strength was important. Leg strength and balance were not a problem but I knew that I was struggling on some of the tasks.

Early one morning in the middle of the third week, I was dragged from my bed, ordered to get dressed, had a hood pulled over my head and my hands tagged behind my back before being pulled and pushed along for at least ten minutes. Outdoors, indoors, out again – I hadn't a clue where I was. Eventually I was shoved into a room and sat down forcibly on a wooden bench. Even though I knew it was an exercise and that no real harm would come to me, it was hard to take.

Before continuing with my story, it might be useful at this stage to explain how I found myself to be there. Every Legionnaire, after all, has his own reasons for seeking such an extreme way of life. For some it is pure adventure, while others are running away from reality or believe that the Legion is just waiting for them to turn up at the door. Whatever the reason, those who are selected are in the minority and I considered myself to be one of the lucky ones to have had the honour of being where I was.

CHAPTER 2

Bygone Days

On 10 June 1983, I found myself in Paris asking a gendarme how to go about joining the French Foreign Legion. He advised me to go home, but realizing that I was intent on enlisting, he told me that I would find a recruiting poster in every main railway station in Paris. I therefore went to the Gare du Nord and sure enough, there was a giant poster advertising an exciting new life in the Legion. It was quite a step to take at the age of thirty-eight and I didn't know if I would be accepted. All my life I had experienced one adventure after another – most of them enjoyable, some disastrous, but nothing on this scale. I have always striven to be the best at whatever I do but suffered from two handicaps – the second of which was a direct result of the first.

When I was at school, dyslexia was unheard of. I was marked down and considered to be slow, almost backward, in some of my teachers' minds. I knew from an early age that this was not the case and I was determined that I would make the most of what I could do well. I knew, even if everyone else didn't, that I had a good brain and that I could learn in time to compensate for my handicap. I also discovered that I had an exceptional eye for detail and could apply logic to tackle the problems I faced.

My second handicap was lack of confidence caused by being told regularly, 'Don't be stupid, you can't do that.' This was to have a profound effect on me for many years. My parents blocked any ambitions I might have had because they thought that I would fail and cause them embarrassment.

Sport was one avenue of release for me and from my early teens I enjoyed success through physical achievement. By the age of fifteen I was house captain, played in the school football team, was school sports champion and represented my country at athletics. I also held the Scottish record for the long jump in my age group.

My main interest was art and I was fortunate that at my school I had two excellent art teachers. I saw this as my future and wanted to go to art school, but my father did not believe that this was a 'real' job and my mother came out with the now familiar phrase 'Don't be stupid, you can't do that.' As a result, I found myself working as 'the post boy' in the office of a wholesale warehouse in Glasgow, which was very unexciting and I knew that I wouldn't stick it out for long. Because I knew that my parents did not agree with my ambitions to become an artist I decided to take my destiny into my own hands – I suppose I 'ran away from home'.

At the tender age of seventeen, I went to London without telling anyone and found myself a job as a junior artist in an advertising agency. I found myself in a shared flat with no friends and very little money, but for the first time in my life I was independent and very happy. It was tough at first, but I learned a lot about my chosen career and, more importantly, about myself.

After a year, my employer opened an office in Glasgow and I decided to move back home. My parents still did not approve of my choice of career, but I was determined to get to the top if only to prove them wrong. To further my skills I enrolled at the Glasgow School of Art for evening classes, five nights a week. I studied graphic and interior design and continued my studies for five years. I have only praise for the quality of my teachers and of the courses. I tried to vary my career by moving from advertising into exhibition stand design, packaging, then back into advertising. The reaction of my parents to my progress did not change – each promotion brought the habitual response, 'Don't be stupid, you can't do that.'

If my promotion achieved a mention in the press they would say, 'How embarrassing, people will be laughing at us.' They refused to accept that I was actually capable and qualified to hold the positions. By the late 1970s I had been appointed Advertising Manager of one of the largest retail groups in the UK. I was now married and had moved to Aberdeen. The group I worked for was going through some major changes due to the sudden death of its owner, so I decided that as I was now using a fountain pen more than my drawing one, it was time for another change.

From the age of fifteen, I had thought about what it would be like to be a policeman, and had even applied to become a police cadet, but in those days the minimum height was 5 foot 9 inches in your stockinged feet, and I had been an inch short. I was friends with a senior officer in Aberdeen City Police and had helped them out on occasions if they needed the help of an artist. He persuaded me that I could use my skills within the force, so I thought why not, and became a police officer.

I loved it. You never knew what was going to happen next. The training was professional and I would have the opportunity to use my specialist skills in a completely different environment once I had completed my two year probationary period. I enjoyed the interaction with the public, having to make on-the-spot decisions that could affect or even save a life.

I was taught first aid, advanced driving skills, how to take control of various situations from football crowd control to major emergencies. I quickly learned that no matter how little service you have, the public look at the uniform and expect you to take charge. I even had the privilege of helping to deliver two babies. I was twenty-four when I decided to join and despite my first handicap, dyslexia, which was more of less unheard of at the time, I managed to pass the entrance examination and started out on my new adventure.

I had no preconceived ideas about what being a police officer would entail, but I was looking forward to a career where every day would be different. The first thing to learn was to take responsibility for your actions. Such responsibility comes as a bit of a shock, but with good professional guidance I soon learned to cope. It was an exciting challenge. Aberdeen City Police had its own training department which covered basic instruction on subjects such as Scottish Criminal Law, The Road Traffic Act and local by-laws. It was a lot to take in on top of the practicalities of the job and was quite stressful at times.

Every new constable served a two-year probationary period which included two, month-long, residential courses at the Scottish Police College which was located in Tullialan Castle in Fife. It was only at the end of the second course that you qualified to be a police officer. Despite Aberdeen having a large student population, the problem of drug and alcohol abuse had never been of major concern, but overnight they became a major problem.

Towards the end of my probationary period, my artistic skills had started to be used by the force's Identification Branch. I became involved in developing a new 'photofit system' and produced some images of suspects that led directly to the arrest of the guilty parties. After one of my images had been released to the press, the culprit came forward voluntarily when his friends and workmates commented jokingly on his likeness to the wanted person. I found myself involved in everything from simple house break-ins, hit-and-run car accidents and sexual assaults, to murder. It opened my eyes to a world that I didn't know existed. From the bizarre to the farcical, from the intriguing to the obscene – I saw it all.

A couple of examples are worthy of a mention. I cannot identify the actual incidents for obvious reasons, but I can explain my involvement. One involved a teenager who said he had been attacked by a gang and had had some words cut into his chest with an open razor. When I photographed his injuries I had the chance to examine them more closely and noticed that the cuts were deeper at the bottom of each stroke. I was able to demonstrate on a pig's carcass that if they had been inflicted by someone standing in front of him as he claimed, the cuts would have been deeper at the beginning of each stroke. When I put it to him that the injuries could not have been inflicted as he described, he eventually admitted that the cuts were self-inflicted in an attempt to get the attention of his parents who doted on his elder brother who was . . . a police officer.

Another case involved an elderly lady who was a resident in a care home and had been subjected to a particularly vicious sexual attack. She had been beaten about the face and her attacker had bitten her on her breasts, severely enough for me to take a cast of one of the wounds. A suspect had been detained but this was in the days before DNA testing and the enquiry was going nowhere. I brought an apple into the interview room and laid it on the table. As the suspect became more confident that we had no evidence, he asked if he could have the apple. Without thinking he took a bite out of it and before he knew what was happening I removed it from his hand and took it to the lab. The imprint of his teeth in the apple matched those that I had cast from the old lady's chest. Got 'im!

I could write a book about my time in the Police but now is not the time. Although I was enjoying the challenges, dedication to the job is not easy on married officers and my marriage was on the rocks. My wife had a full-time job and as a result we hardly saw each other. I found myself looking for alternative ways to spend my off-duty hours and decided to take up another challenge – flying.

This was everything I had dreamed it would be and I threw myself into it body and soul. The joys of flying cannot be put into words – it has to be experienced for oneself.

Single engine, multi-engine, helicopters, night flying, instrument flying, aerobatics, I did them all, but nothing compared to the thrill of my first solo. That was definitely one of the high points of my life. My instructor had just landed with me and as we taxied back to the holding point ready to re-enter the runway, he opened the door without warning, jumped out and shouted, 'Off you go. You're on your own.'

I hadn't had a chance to think about it so I wasn't nervous. The control tower had been advised in advance and the circuit had been cleared of all other traffic. I made my take-off and was about to turn on to the approach when I heard an inbound commercial flight's call that it was coming in to land. Normally commercial aircraft have priority, but he was told to wait until I had landed as I was on a first solo flight. When I called in that I had cleared the runway, the pilot of the inbound jet congratulated me and arranged to meet me in the airport bar afterwards. I was on a high.

With Aberdeen now being the European oil capital, the airport was expanding from a couple of Porticabins to being an international airport. A brand-new terminal was under construction and a police unit was being formed to work in it. I had been in the Police for just over seven years and leapt at the chance to combine my new hobby with my work. I had enjoyed my time as a detective but volunteered to go back into uniform to take on yet another challenge.

Being back on regular shift work enabled me to continue flying so I was spending more and more time at the airport. This was not helping my home life which was by now in free fall to disaster. I was moonlighting with some of the air taxi companies which was against police regulations and I knew that I was pushing my luck. I was able to undertake short-flight aircraft transfers for the airlines, saving them using up expensive and valuable commercial pilot flight hours. I would fly before or after a shift so it was only a matter of time before I got stranded somewhere because of weather or a mechanical breakdown. I wasn't doing it for the money, although it paid well – it was the adventure that drew me and perhaps the knowledge that I was bucking the system. My shift system gave me long weekends off and I was able to use them to move aircraft greater distances – Norway, the Channel Islands, Western Europe, my flights were getting further and the aircraft larger, but times were changing. I had never made the transition to jet aircraft and even the smaller companies were now buying the new range of small short-haul jets that had come on the market. There were fewer piston aircraft for me to fly.

My wife thought that my ever-increasing absences were due to me having an affair and I did nothing to change this view. It was obvious that we could not continue like this. After a serious talk about our future, it was decided that a complete change of environment was our only chance if we were to save our marriage. My wife wanted to move back to our home area to be nearer her family, so I applied for a transfer from Aberdeen (now Grampian) to Strathclyde Police.

We made the move in 1980 – new location, new challenges, new adventures – and I never flew an aircraft again. Things were fine for a while on the marital front and I had lots to occupy me with settling into a new home and job. After a brief period in uniform on the west side of Glasgow, I was transferred to Police HQ where I was attached to the press public relations department and the photographic unit.

The force was organizing an international police tattoo, with participants coming from all over the world. My old marketing skills were put to use and I enjoyed being part of the production team. The event was a great success and we filled the Kelvinhall Arena every night for a week; the final performance was televised and everyone was happy.

With this brief bit of excitement over I quickly became bored. Home life had not improved and my wife and I had grown apart. Who was to blame? Probably me. I know that one always thinks that it is the fault of the other person but I must accept honestly that I was the main problem. I have this need to be always finding new challenges – I can't sit at home and do nothing. I must have made life miserable for my wife.

Eventually I started drinking although I don't remember how it started. I had not been teetotal, but very rarely drank and never went into a bar on my own. This of course only made things worse. I had always been fit, played football, squash and golf, swam and regularly went running. Sporting facilities within the Police were excellent and we were encouraged to use them. Drinking was just not me.

In the end, things came to a head at home and I decided to leave. It had been a mistake to think that our problems could be solved by simply moving to another area, on top of which I was not happy at work. Aberdeen City Police was a great force, with an excellent officer structure and good honest policing methods. Perhaps it was the pure size of Strathclyde, for there are many very good, efficient, honest officers within its ranks, but there were some, albeit a minority, who were not. The Police, like every other walk of life, are only human. In a workforce that runs into thousands there is bound to be a small percentage who are incompetent or downright dishonest. The combination of my own personal problems and some of the people I was working with made me decide to resign. It was time to move on to another adventure.

I have never regretted my years as a police officer, they were great, and I learned so much about life, including the realization that there are few of us mortals who do not experience major problems at some time in our lives. Being a police officer teaches one to deal with other people's problems in a sympathetic way. Ninety per cent of a police officer's time is spent helping others – locking up offenders occupies only a small part of the working day. It is when officers don't have time to spend on the first part that police public relations break down and the crime rate soars. I will describe later how this early grounding helped me deal with more dramatic circumstances.

For the next eighteen months I was at an all-time low. I was never out of work, but everything was an anti-climax after the previous ten years. It was not that the work I was doing was uninteresting, far from it. I was managing and marketing a new Scottish quality timeshare holiday complex, but my personal life was a mess. I had stopped drinking and I was getting back my old level of fitness, but I needed more than this, so I moved on again in search of I knew not what.

It was during this period that my father died suddenly in hospital in circumstances that led to a public enquiry. It was a distressing time for all the family, in particular my mother who, like many of her generation, had never had to deal with the problems of daily life, such as paying the bills. She had not spent one day on her own in her whole life and took her anger and frustrations out on the only person who was there to help her. 'This is all your fault', 'If it wasn't for you doing this or that' – on and on it went.

I was now thirty-seven and had lost all belief in myself. I was at rock bottom. It is amazing how you can go from success to failure in such a short time. I couldn't hold a job down and had become homeless. I needed a roof over my head so I set out to walk from Edinburgh, where I found myself, to Prestwick where my mother lived. I got a couple of lifts but walked most of the way. It seemed hard at the time but it was nothing to the walking I would do over the following eleven years. I eventually got to my mother's house and thankfully she said that I could stay until I got myself sorted out. At least I was able to paint and sold enough of my work to put a few pounds in my pocket. But my mother was finding it hard to adapt to her loss and my presence was not making it any easier for her. Relations were strained, to say the least, and I became depressed, seeing no end to my present circumstances.

At the beginning of June 1983, I decided that I had had enough. I went out and bought a litre bottle of whisky and walked to the beach which stretches for over 5 miles from Prestwick to Troon. It has high sand dunes and is normally deserted except for a few people walking their dogs along the shoreline.

There was plenty of driftwood and I set about gathering large pieces to make a shelter in the dunes, which I then covered with grass and sand. It was totally hidden from the waterline and would only be discovered by someone who came into the gully I had chosen. I was very focused about what I was about to do and can remember every moment clearly to this day. I went into my little hide at about 5.00 pm and drank the whole bottle of whisky in about fifteen minutes. At first it was hard to swallow but as the effect of the whisky set in it became easier and soon the bottle was empty. I could see out to sea and watched a magnificent sunset over the Isle of Arran before I must have passed out.

When I came round it was just after 2.00 pm on the Saturday. I had been out for over forty hours. It had been Thursday afternoon when I had come down to the beach and what brought me round was the constant roar of aircraft. It was the afternoon of the Scottish Air Show at Prestwick Airport and the end of the runway was less than half a mile away, in a direct line with my place of concealment.

At first I could not remember what had happened or where I was, but then I was violently sick. This continued for some time until I was dry retching. I had the hangover of all time and I think I fell asleep again for a couple of hours. I was eventually tempted out of my hide by the sound of aircraft performing aerobatics above my head and couldn't resist having a look. It was a warm June afternoon and when I emerged I was surprised to find a group of people standing less than 10 feet away at the top of the dunes. I must have looked a mess – I had two days' growth of beard and felt like a tramp. They looked at me with disgust, but no one asked me if was all right.

I stood and watched the displays for a while and soon warmed up in the afternoon sun. Eventually I made my way back to the house where, despite my state, my mother said nothing and went into the kitchen. She didn't ask me where I had been or if I was all right. All she said was, 'I hope the neighbours didn't see you.'

That made my mind up to go. I didn't know where but it was like all those years ago when I was seventeen. I had gone then and succeeded – I could do it again.

I had saved a bit of money, but would have to be careful. I went to my room, had a shower and a shave, packed a bag with the bare essentials, picked up my passport and went back through to the living room. I told my mother I was leaving but all she said was, 'Make sure you leave your key,' before turning back to the kitchen. I walked out of the door without looking back.

I still had no idea where I was going or what I was going to do. As it was summer, I thought I might go down to the South of France and try my hand selling my paintings direct to the public.

There was a direct bus service from Ayr, via Kilmarnock, to Dover and I was able to join the bus at Prestwick. It was a long overnight ride but I slept most of the way and felt refreshed by the time I caught the ferry to Calais. I was ready for my new adventure.

I had never been to France before and didn't speak a word of French. Like most Brits I assumed that everyone else spoke English – how arrogant we are!

My next stop was Paris and I fell in love with it immediately. London may be a great city, and there are many impressive buildings and places of interest to visit, but nothing prepares you for the beauty of Paris. I decided to spend some time doing the tourist bit and it was easy to find a cheap, clean hotel right in the heart of the city. Two days later I found myself in an Irish pub and got speaking to a couple of English-speaking lads. One was Swiss and the other Australian. Both were tanned and well built, and told me that they were on leave from the French Foreign Legion, having spent the past two years in French Guyana in South America. They were just starting a month's leave before heading back to the Legion HQ at Aubagne in the South of France, where they would be posted to a new regiment. They did not glamorize the life but from what they told me they obviously enjoyed what they did. I realized that at thirty-eight I was probably too old but they said that the age limit was forty and they had sparked that old sense of adventure in me.

When I eventually got to bed in the early hours of the morning, I couldn't sleep. My mind was racing and I knew that my mind was made up – nothing ventured, nothing gained.

I rose early, had breakfast and set off on the next part of my life. I had no idea what was in store for me, but it couldn't be worse than trying to commit suicide on a beach.

CHAPTER 3

Into the Unknown

There was a telephone number on the recruitment poster and I was encouraged by the fact that the poster was in English. What I didn't know was that the posters were printed in the language most commonly used by persons arriving at a particular railway station. When I phoned the number, someone spoke to me in what passed for English and gave me directions to the recruitment centre for Paris at Fort du Nogent on the eastern outskirts of Paris. I found my way there and was soon standing outside the massive doors of an ancient fort dating back to Napoleonic times. The fort itself was awesome and just plucking up the courage to ring the doorbell is, in itself, the first obstacle to joining the Legion. I am sure that quite a few get cold feet at that point and turn away.

A small wicket gate set into the huge doors swung open in response to my ring although I had not heard the bell. The sentry was dressed in green combat fatigues but was wearing the famous white kepi that is associated with the Legion. I was shown into the guardroom and told to sit on a wooden bench. Eventually someone who I thought was a sergeant came out and asked what I wanted. I explained why I was there, thinking that I was special – little did I know that he heard this sort of thing dozens of times a day. I was to find out later that if he didn't like a person for any reason they would be shown the door and that would be that. He noted my name and asked if I had any proof of identity. I handed him my passport and I saw his eyes stop at my date of birth. He looked down at me, shrugged his shoulders and said that I was a bit old for this sort of thing. Instead of showing me the door, he shouted for one of the guards to escort me to another area of the fort.

We walked across the fort to another building before being shown into an other room where six other lads, all much younger than me, were seated on benches, stripped to their underwear. None of them said anything, and I was instructed in a mixture of French and sign language to get my clothes off and take a seat.

After about half an hour of waiting in what was not a warm room, a medic called us into an examination room one by one. A doctor performed a basic medical examination, checking the curvature of the spine, heart, lungs, teeth, ears and eyesight. He spoke no English and I was aware of a second person observing my attitude and ability to work out what I was being asked to do. The whole thing took less than ten minutes and I found myself back in the waiting room still in my underwear. Another lad had arrived and was immediately sent in to be examined. When the new arrival came back out, four of our group were told to get back into their clothes and were taken away. We never saw them again.

No words had been exchanged between us and I had no idea what nationality any of the others were. Those of us remaining, including myself, were taken into another room and issued with a plain green tracksuit, a pair of blue trainers and a basic uniform, which consisted of a pair of black shoes, black socks, khaki shirt, green tie and beret, and a brown jacket and trousers, a bit like my old police uniform. We were also given clean underwear which we had to put on. There were no badges or insignia of any kind on either the uniform or the beret.

Having been thus kitted out, we were told to put on the tracksuit, socks and trainers. Everything else, including our own clothes, was put in a kitbag. All our private documents, wallets and money were take from us, sealed in envelopes and taken away. It felt like we were going to prison.

Next we were taken to a large barrack room where we were allocated a bunk bed and a locker to stow the kitbags in. We were also given a basic toilet kit of soap, razor, toothpaste and toothbrush. There were twenty-eight others already in the room, which I estimated could sleep up to fifty – basic accommodation but very clean.

We were left to make our own introductions amongst ourselves. Some of the lads had already been there for almost a week and had formed small groups according to nationality or ability to communicate in a common language. There were several German speakers, one Swede who spoke good English, a couple of black Africans who kept to themselves, some French speakers and a group comprising a Canadian, a New Zealander, a Pole, a fellow Scot and two lads from England. The one thing that was obvious was that I was considerably older than any of them.

At about six in the evening we were taken to a mess room and fed. The food was basic but nutritious and we were given a glass of red wine with the meal. The wine, it was pointed out, came from the Legion's own vineyards at Puyloubier in the South of France.

After the meal we were led to the kitchens and put to work cleaning the dishes. You get nothing for nothing in the Legion and as we were to find out, there are no civilian staff in it. Everything from cooking to general maintenance is done by the legionnaires themselves. We finished our chores at about 8.00 pm and were taken back to our barrack room. There then followed a two-hour film about the Legion of yesteryear and today. Being someone who knew nothing about the Legion – and I suspected that I was not the only one – I found it fascinating. We still didn't have a clue as to what was going to happen next. Were we now in the Legion? Where and what kind of instruction were we going to get? I had no idea.

After this introduction it was explained that we would be travelling by train to Aubagne the following morning. We learned that the headquarters of the Legion were just outside Marseille and that it would be there that we would undergo the selection process. Today had just been the first step in the process; the real thing was still to come.

We would travel in the uniforms we had been issued with and were warned that although we would be travelling on public transport, we were not to talk to anyone on the journey. To do so would mean being shown the door when we got to our destination.

It became obvious to me that many of my new companions were trying to outdo each other in their claims about what they had done before. Everything from previous military experience to physical ability was bragged about, most of which could be taken with a pinch of salt. Gaining entry was going to be very competitive and there was a dog-eat-dog atmosphere creeping in even at this early stage. I had a feeling that this was quite the opposite of what the Legion was all about.

After an early breakfast and the mandatory dishwashing, we set off by coach for the station. We must have looked a strange bunch as we were led onto the train – more like a bunch of criminals than elite soldiers, and perhaps a few of us were, if the truth be known.

The journey was uneventful and I was beginning to realize just how big a country France is. The population of the UK and France may be the same, but there the comparison ends. I enjoy travelling and fortunately it was daylight so I was able to see the changing countryside as we made our way south towards the Méditerranée. My spirits were up and it was hard to believe that I had been at such a low ebb exactly seven days earlier. Life is a strange affair.

Apart from being the selection centre for the Legion, Aubagne is also the place through which all Legion personnel pass on their way to and from a posting, on a course or for medical treatment. It is the hub of everything that happens within the Legion, including administration. The selection centre of the Legion is like no other in any army. Your length of stay there can vary from a couple of hours to several weeks. During your stay there you are locked in behind a 3-metre-high fence topped with razor wire. You can ask to leave at any time during your stay and will have all your belongings returned to you before you are taken to your port of entry to France and deported. You are also given enough money to assure your immediate needs for the journey. I was astonished to discover that there were 200 other young men in the centre going through the selection process.

Our uniforms were taken away from us and we were left with our tracksuits, a change of underwear and of course the regulation black socks and blue trainers; the only time we were allowed out of the compound was to go to the camp infirmary for various medicals. The accommodation was modern if basic and spread over three floors. New arrivals were accommodated on the top floor in one large barrack room, with bunk beds stacked three high. We had no clothes or possessions so we did not need a locker. Our change of underwear, toothbrush and toiletries were kept in a small bag which we hung on the end of our bed. There was a large exercise yard with some keep-fit equipment and a Nissen hut type of building to shelter in if the weather was bad. There were also two classrooms where some of the tests took place.

On the day of our arrival we were taken to the infirmary where we were given a very thorough medical, including x-rays, to confirm that we were healthy and carried no ailments that could spread to others in such crowded conditions. We were also examined to ensure that we were not homosexual or carrying any sexual diseases. If you didn't like it you could leave. We had been joined by others who had arrived from other recruiting centres, including those who walked up to the gates of Aubagne.

There were seventy-five of us who attended the infirmary that first day and on our return we were already down to fifty. We were given yellow armbands and it was explained that the aim was to progress through selection on to the second floor where we would be given a red armband. We were locked out of the building from 8.00 am to 5.00 pm every day and had to amuse ourselves in the yard when we were not undergoing one test or another.

The following day, the next step in the induction process started. The French Army has a security service called the Deuxième Bureau, or B2, amongst whose functions is the security evaluation of all military personnel. They are responsible for all levels of clearance throughout your military career, but should not be confused with the French Secret Service, the DST. My first interview was carried out by an English NCO in the Legion. I was asked to confirm the information I had already provided and to write the equivalent of a CV, including everything about my personal background. No other questions were asked at this stage of the procedure and I was shown back to the compound.

The following day nothing happened and I spent the day people watching. My fellow applicants were of all shapes and sizes, religions, nationalities and social backgrounds. There were certainly some ex-military amongst them, but most were there for a variety of reasons, ranging from escaping from political upheaval in their own country to unemployment, or from personal problems such as a marital breakdown. There were bound to be some who had a criminal background but the system was designed to weed them out.

A few were from the French colonies such as Tahiti and were looked on favourably. A small percentage were there because of the Legion's reputation and looked upon themselves as super heroes. An even smaller number wanted to be mercenary soldiers and considered themselves as ultimate killers. Most of these were gone after the first interview. I noticed that the number of lads in our original group was going down rapidly by the hour, but that they were quickly being replaced by newcomers.

The following day I was recalled by the B2 and asked to write my history again. This is a tactic used by the police worldwide to check the authenticity of the original statement. Very few people who have made up the first version can remember what they said the first time in every detail. Half an hour after I had finished I was called back into the room and asked about my police career. They had confirmed that I had told the truth through Interpol but were concerned that I had been sent to seek out the identities of UK nationals who might have taken refuge in the Legion.

After several hours of fairly intensive interrogation I was left alone for five minutes before being told to return to the compound. I thought that I was going to be rejected at that point but instead was taken to the second floor and given a red armband. I had passed to the next stage.

The following morning I went back to the infirmary to get the results of my blood tests. Everything was fine and that afternoon I started a series of IQ tests. These are given to each candidate in his own language and I found them pretty easy. I knew that I wouldn't have any problem with this side of the selection process. During the next couple of days I made friends with a Canadian, a South African, a Vietnamese and a Japanese. We would become very close friends over the coming years.

A fortnight after entering the recruitment centre I was called to see the officer in charge. He advised me that I had passed initial selection and would leave for the training regiment at Castelnaudary near Toulouse in a few days – if I wished to continue. This would be my last chance to walk away before signing a five-year contract. I was also asked if I wished to change my name. This is a Legion tradition which goes back to its time of conception. If you choose to do so, your old identity will cease to exist within the Legion from that moment. The Legion will protect your anonymity under a code of honour that cannot be broken by either party. If a Legionnaire were to reveal his old identity or presence in the Legion to anyone, the Legion would consider the agreement broken and would immediately withdraw their protection. Under the rules, if a man's new name was Fred Bloggs, any enquiry about his real name would be rebuffed. The man's real name would only be known to the B2 – all his paperwork, including his contract of engagement, would be in his new name. Even the commanding officer of his regiment would not know his real name, although the B2 security officer attached to the regiment would have access to his file.

I had no reason to change my name but it was suggested that due to my age it might be easier for me if they changed my date of birth. Future instructors might go easier on me if I lost ten years of my age, so at the stroke of a pen I went from thirty-eight to twenty-eight. Oh, if only it was so easy physically.

From my initial group of seventy-five, we were now down to just eight. We moved to the ground floor and joined another twelve who were waiting for the numbers to be made up before heading for the training regiment. Although I had signed a five-year contract, in French, I was still not a Legionnaire. I thought I was, but I wasn't. We were called 'Engagé Voluntaires'. None of us knew that what we had just signed was an agreement that if we passed the instruction at Castelnaudary, the five-year contract would be valid. We had not only signed an agreement that gave them the right to kick us out at any time up to that point, without notice or explanation, but we also retained the right to ask to leave during the same period. If this had been explained to us it might have stopped some lads deserting. It was all there in black and white, but even those who could read French didn't look at the small print.

At the end of the day, the Legion wanted to be the ones who decided who should stay and who should go. After all it was the Legion that was spending the money on our upkeep and instruction. Luckily for me, all my new friends had made it this far and we would soon learn to help each other through the months to come. We were kitted out for the journey and were told to sign our personal clothes and possessions over to the Legion. They would be kept in a store until we passed out, but after that the Legion could dispose of them as they wished. I still had £150 worth of French Francs which were put into a Post Office account and the book kept by the B2.

CHAPTER 4

Basic Instruction

Castelnaudary is a small agricultural market town about 15 miles from the second city of France, Toulouse. It is a very fertile area and there are many famous vineyards in the region. It also supports one of the largest cooperative storage systems in Europe and the Canal du Midi flows through the centre of the town. Although the immediate area round the town is flat, the Pyrenees are only a stone's throw away.

In my time, the actual camp was situated in the heart of the old town, but a new modern camp has now been built a couple of miles south of the town and has all the facilities you require to train a modern army. The original barracks were built at the turn of the century and it was not until the 1960s that it was taken over by the Legion. It was typical of old army camps throughout France and although the accommodation was adequate, it was far from modern.

The 'caserne' (barracks) comprised two large four-storey buildings that would have passed for prison blocks, on either side of the parade square. There were several slightly newer secondary buildings within the compound, which was surrounded by a 20-foot-high concrete wall topped with barbed wire. The two main buildings were divided into four instruction companies and a command company. There were a further two basic instruction companies based in old farms which lay a couple of miles outside the town.

We travelled from Aubagne to Castelnaudary by train, and again I enjoyed seeing more of France as we made our way along the coast towards Spain before heading inland towards Toulouse. Half an hour before we got to our destination, we passed the medieval town of Carcassonne, with its high walls and pointed towers. There is nothing like that in the UK.

On our arrival we were lined up on the parade square and from that moment on all orders and instruction was given in French. We were forbidden to speak our own languages during the working day – to do so would lead to a punishment. We were joined by forty other recruits who had been waiting for our arrival before beginning instruction.

They started to split us into two companies of thirty, and again my luck held when my new friends were assigned to the same company. We were then paired up with a French speaker who became your partner, or 'benom', for the rest of our instruction. My benom was called Thomas, who was actually French and had served in the Navy during his national service, which still existed in France. He spoke a little English but the idea was that you would pick up enough French to enable you to understand the basics quickly. Surnames were used all the time by the instructors and strangely this would become the common way of addressing even our friends. French nationals are not supposed to be able to join the Legion so most of them say that they come from French-speaking countries such as Monaco, Switzerland and even Canada.

We were issued with our full kit and I was impressed by the fact that everything was brand new. The idea was that you were responsible for keeping your equipment in good condition and had to account for any abnormal breakages or deterioration. There was method in their madness.

I had always thought of myself as being fit but I had no idea what real fitness was. I was to discover depths of personal endurance that would help me go on long after I would normally have given up.

The best news of all was that we were being sent to one of the farms to undergo our instruction – it had to be better than being confined inside the barracks. We were fed and watered, and spent the first night at the main camp. It had been a long day and I was glad to get my head down early before having a good night's sleep.

The following morning we were up at the crack of dawn and breakfasted before setting out for the farm. This would be home for the next four months and I was keen to get on with it. I knew that it was going to be tough going, but it was what I needed in my life at that moment.

The farm buildings had been converted and adapted for use as a military training camp. The large stone barn had been converted into our quarters, with the ground floor used for storage of our equipment and a classroom for indoor instruction. The loft had been turned into our accommodation with the use of classic camp beds. With its high wooden roof and spacious feeling, it was perfect for the job. There was a stairway but we were forbidden to use it unless we were carrying equipment. The only other access was by climbing or descending a rope attached to the old barn hoist, which would have been used to lift straw bales up to the top floor. My first attempts at climbing the rope were pathetic and I had to learn the technique. We soon learned that it was not about pure muscle power – there is an easy way and a hard way to do everything, and this was no exception. By the end of our time at the farm I could go up and down that rope like a circus act, without using my feet – but then so could everyone else, for that matter.

It was rare that we were indoors and the grounds were extensive with every type of terrain you could imagine. There was open ground, woodlands and a ravine with a fast-flowing river winding its way through it. There was even a deserted village that had been adapted for use as an urban combat complex, and an obstacle course that had been designed to test speed, agility and strength. This course was identical in every military camp in France and the national records for its completion by a group or individual were held by the Legion. At first I was just pleased to get round it, but after a while I found myself racing against the clock, never mind the guy next to me.

There was also a football/rugby pitch and our overall fitness was helped along with daily 15-kilometre runs in sports kit or 8 kilometres in combats. I found that my age was actually a plus factor as I had a certain stamina that was lacking in the younger lads. I was having no trouble keeping up with the physical programme, and if anything was stronger overall than most. My weak point was my arm strength, but that was improving every day.

I was enjoying every minute of it, throwing myself into every challenge that came my way, and there was plenty of mental stimulation as well. I was also picking up more and more French every day with the help of my benom. Every night I went to sleep exhausted but contented. Any sign of depression had been banished for good. I was literally a changed man, healthy and proud of my achievements. There was no one telling me, 'Don't be stupid, you can't do that.'

The farmyard was our parade ground and we had to learn the slow marching style that is unique to the Legion. It is more of a swagger compared to the stiff marching style of the British Army, and there were also the marching songs that proclaim the glorious history of the Legion. We had to sing every night, which was also an enjoyable way to improve our French.

After a couple of weeks we had our first drop-outs. The physical training and instruction methods used by the Legion were designed to weed out the weak as soon as possible. We were subjected to some pretty harsh treatment with what seemed at the time as pointless repetitive group punishment. Some cracked and left, either officially by the front door or by deserting at night. Sometimes it was difficult to decide which was which as one moment they would be there, the next never to be seen again. It was impossible to find out the truth and rumours about what had happened to them were rife

– everything from heroic tales of how the person had evaded capture, that they had been caught and were being tortured in a dungeon somewhere, to tales that they had been shot. The more extreme the story the happier our instructors were and they did nothing to make us think differently. It was all part of the legend. What was happening was that there was a bonding of those who remained and our energies were being directed, without us knowing, it into strong groups who worked together for each other. The reality was that we were being manipulated by experts – it was they who were in complete control.

As our training progressed, there were subtle changes in the instructors' methods and our new-found strengths were used to form groups which could rely on each other, drawing on individual strengths. It showed us the power that exists within a well-bonded group as individuals began to demonstrate leadership qualities within the group. We believed that it was us who were beginning to beat the system, thinking that we were special, an elite group who were better than those who had passed this way before us. We were now working and thinking like soldiers determined to achieve the tasks set us.

After two months of non-stop effort, seven days a week of intensive instruction, we returned to the main camp for our first bit of freedom since we walked into the recruiting centres. We were given a four-hour pass to go into town. For the first five years of your service, dress uniform has to be worn in town by all Legionnaires below the rank of Caporal Chef. At this stage we still wore a beret, not a kepi, which made us stand out against the 'real' Legionnaires, but we were still proud to wear the uniform.

That first evening in town might have been expected to turn into a drunken release of pent-up emotions. In fact, most of us went and had a slap-up meal and a couple of beers before heading back to camp half an hour before we were due back. No one turned up late or the worse for drink. Later on there were some who succumbed to temptation, but for now we all had a new-found pride in ourselves as individuals and as a group.

Another milestone had been passed and when we returned to the farm on the Monday morning, we were ready to tackle the next part of our training.

It was not only our attitudes that had changed – the teaching methods and aims moved up a gear. If we thought that we had reached the peak of fitness and tolerance to extreme conditions, were we sadly mistaken. The length and pace of the marches increased, and combat exercises doubled in intensity and duration, with little or no sleep. Each combat group was now working as a team, with unit achievement more important than individual.

Inter-group rivalry was intense and there was a league table, with points being awarded for all aspects of military knowledge. As the instructors raised the pace, the numbers of those dropping out increased accordingly.

We were rapidly approaching the end of our third month and with it an event that would change our lives for ever and stay imprinted in our memories for the rest of our lives – making the transition from 'Engagé Voluntaire' to being a 'Legionnaire'.

A week of practical and written tests covering everything from shooting, weapons, explosives and mines, combat tactics, map reading, signals, first aid, maths and French, led up to the final endurance test known as 'The Kepi March'. This was a four-day forced march with combat objectives and ambushes day and night. The route covered every type of terrain imaginable and was a real test of physical and mental endurance.

On the final day of the march we got back to the farm at about 10.00 in the evening. With everyone almost out on their feet, we noticed that the farmyard/parade square was lit by tins filled with oil. Of the thirty of us who had started out on the training together, only twenty of us were left. All my friends had made it through, even though we were not all in the same combat groups. Up until now we had only touched the famous white kepi when we were fitted for them on our last weekend at Castelnaudary. They had then been put in plastic bags, labelled with our names and taken from us. Over the past couple of weeks we had been learning by heart to recite the 'Legion Code of Honour', but had not realized just how important and moving a ceremony it would be.

We were lined up before our Captain and the Colonel of the training regiment to begin the ceremony that would turn us into Legionnaires. After a short speech by the Colonel, we were asked to repeat the 'Code of Honour' in unison. At the end the Colonel gave the order 'Remise de la kepi'. As one, we removed the green beret with our left hand, put it into the left trouser pocket, placed the kepi on our heads with the right hand and saluted. These movements were all done in silence.

I was now a Legionnaire.

We celebrated our new status that night with more than a few beers and lots of traditional singing. We were all on a high and the fatigue of the last four hours was forgotten . . . for the moment.

The following day we had an unheard of lie-in, didn't get up until eight and the day was spent cleaning and checking our equipment. We still had another month of training to go before we would be assigned to a regiment.

When I had started out on this challenge I had known that there was a distinct possibility that a percentage of my fellow recruits might be violent criminals, thieves, drug users or bullies. I now felt confident that these men, who were my brothers in arms, were made of better stuff, and if they had dubious backgrounds, they were changed men.

The selection system and training was designed to weed out the wrong type of recruit right from the start. Due to the huge number of young men turning up at the gates for selection, and the relatively small number that made it, the Legion could afford to be very selective. The physical, mental and moral standards set guaranteed that most of the undesirables could be eliminated from the start. There will always be a certain number of undesirables who will manage to slip through the system, but few who will stick it out through the rigorous training.

Of the twenty of us left, five were English, two Scots, a South African, a Vietnamese, an Australian, a Swiss, a Swede, a Canadian, a Japanese, two Italians, a Tahitian and three 'French'.

Our time at the farm had come to an end and we moved back to the main camp at Castelnaudary. The remaining instruction was theoretic and included more about the history of the Legion and about today's regiments. What was left of the two companies that had started together were combined, and we were told that whoever finished in the top ten at the end of the month would be given the chance to choose which regiment they wanted to go to. I did not have any particular preference and had assumed that at my age I would probably end up in administration.

By now it was the end of October 1983 and it was becoming colder by the day. We continued to have weekly tests which were designed to test our aptitude for different specialities such as signals, medics, vehicle mechanics or administration. The other choice that would be offered to the top group was to stay behind at Castelnaudary for two years, with an immediate chance to go on an accelerated Caporals' course. It would mean rapid promotion but those selected would only get the chance of going to one of the combat regiments after two years.

When the final results were announced, I could not believe that I was in the leading group along with the names of my closest friends. We talked about it at great length and agreed that if we could we would stick together and apply for the same regiment. The 2eme Regiment Etranger de Parachutistes is the elite of the Legion, so we all asked to go there. I was excited at the prospect and wished to stay with my friends despite my age.

We were interviewed individually and I still expected that my application would be rejected because of my age. I couldn't get it into my head that as far as everyone was concerned I was only twenty-eight – mature but not too old. I am convinced that if my real age had been on my personal documents, I would not have had a chance.

To our delight we were all told that we would be going to the REP and that a further selection process would have to be gone through once we got there.

CHAPTER 5

The 2ème REP

The journey from Castelnaudary to Calvi in Corsica was literally another voyage into the unknown. Everyone retraced their steps by train back to Aubagne where we spent a couple of days completing our administrative documents before continuing our separate ways to our new regiments. We said our goodbyes to the others, knowing we might never see them again, or at least not for a couple of years. While at Aubagne it felt strange looking at all the young men behind the fence of the recruiting centre waiting to find out if they would go on the same voyage of discovery as ourselves. It seemed a lifetime since we had been there too, not four months.

To get to Corsica we had to travel on the overnight ferry from Marseille to Bastia, the largest town on the island. We were escorted by a Caporal Chef and a Caporal who were heading back to the regiment. It was seemingly normal for anyone in transport to perform this duty, even though there was nowhere we could go as we were taken to the port by bus and would be met on the other side to be taken to the camp. It was made clear to us that any misbehaviour would not be tolerated. We were not as yet members of the Regiment and putting a foot wrong would result in the culprit, or all of us for that matter, being sent back to Aubagne.

After being allocated our cabins we gathered on the top deck of the ship to watch our departure out of the legendary port. It was to be a voyage that I would make many times in the future and it would never lose its magic. At exactly 10.00 pm the ship slipped its berth at the Quay Lafayette and the great inner port suddenly lay before us. With the Basilica on our left and the old fort of Saint Jean on the right, the view was magnificent. The old port was illuminated like a Christmas tree and the church high on the hill to our right overlooked the port like a guardian angel.

After the ship had turned round it headed out to sea, passing through the entrance in the breakwater. We were told by someone that we should go to the other side of the deck if we wanted to see one of the most famous places in the Mediterranean – the infamous prison from *The Count of Monte Cristo* on the island of Ratonneau, 'Le Chateau d'If'. It is now a tourist must for anyone visiting Marseille and a small ferry makes the voyage every hour during daylight hours.

We watched the island slip past before going below to one of the lounges for a couple of beers before returning to our cabins for the night. There were four of us to a cabin and although it was very warm the cabins were quite large and well ventilated. Another Scot had joined us from the other section and this was the first time he had been further afield than the east end of Glasgow. Just getting this far had been a monumental experience for him and the tension had been building in him for weeks.

At about four in the morning the Scottish lad suddenly sat up in bed and started screaming. He was sound asleep but was fighting some unseen enemy and thrashing about. We tried to hold him down and in the heat of the moment he bit the ear of one of the lads quite badly. He was hyperventilating and we had to send for the ship's doctor to give him a tranquilizer to calm him down. Most of the passengers on our deck were now awake and goodness knows what they must have been thinking. My friend required a couple of stitches in his ear. When the lad woke up in the morning he did not believe us when we told him what he had done, and did not have any recollection of the incident whatsoever.

We all rose early and went on deck to get our first view of Corsica. None of us had any idea of the terrain or anything else about the island apart from the fact that Napoleon was born there. We watched as the ship rounded the most northern part of the island known as Cap Corse and were impressed by the sheer size and beauty of the mountains which rose straight out of the sea.

When we finally docked at Bastia it was just after 7.00 am. Everyone was looking forward to what the new day would bring and it was obvious at first glance that the island was much larger than we had imagined. All we knew was that Calvi and the Legion camp were on the other side of the island, and that it would take us a couple of hours to get there by bus. Although it was November, it was much warmer than it had been in France – in fact, to us it was downright hot. What must it be like in the middle of summer?

Everything we owned fitted into our kitbags and we were first off the ferry via the car ramp. The military police were waiting for us on the quayside and we were joined by several other Legionnaires who were returning to the Regiment from the Continent. Some had been on leave, some on courses.

Within the hour we had left the port on the Legion bus and were heading out of town towards the foothills of the mountains. The road followed the coast for half an hour before beginning the tortuous journey up into the hills. This was not a road for the faint at heart but our driver was not in the least put off and handled the bus with great skill. At times we were looking down into a vertical drop of over a hundred feet into a fast-flowing river. It took another three quarters of an hour to reach the highest part of the journey and the bus stopped at the top of the pass to allow everyone a quick comfort stop at the roadside.

The pass bridged the spine of the mountain range which ran from tip to toe of the island. Corsica lies on a north-south axis parallel to Italy and although it is now part of France, it is closer to Italy. It was occupied by the Italians at the time of Nelson and the local language is an ancient Italian dialect which is still spoken daily by the indigenous population. The view from the top of the pass was spectacular – you could see all the way to the sea and the ribbons of sand that formed the beautiful beaches were set off by the brilliant turquoise of the sea.

It took us another hour to make the descent to the coast and as we rounded a bend in the village of Lumio, our escorts pointed out the camp which was halfway between where we were and the town of Calvi. Calvi is situated at the far side of a large horseshoe bay and we could clearly make it out, sitting at the foot of the walls of the old Genoese citadel which guards the entrance to the harbour. We were still a couple of hundred feet above sea level and the entire bay was laid out before us like a 3D map.

My life seemed to have been progressing in clearly defined steps over the past six months and I was under no illusion that this next phase was going to be another major step in my life.

Five minutes later we had arrived at the gates of Camp Raffalli. We were now at sea level and the camp was framed by the magnificent, snow-capped mountains. I did not realize that they were almost 3,000 metres in height, twice that of Ben Nevis, the highest mountain in the UK. From the beach to the foothills was less than 15 miles and the mountains seemed to tower over us.

We were taken straight to a single-storey accommodation block which would be our home for the next four weeks. Before being accepted by the Regiment we had to take part in four weeks' parachute training, at the end of which we would have to make a series of jumps to qualify for our jump wings. Only then would we become part of the Regiment.

Despite the snow capping the mountains, the rise in temperature brought it home to us that we were now in the Med. There was a difference of almost 10° Celsius between Castelnaudary and Calvi, and the sky was a shade of blue that I had only seen in travel brochures.

It turned out that there were already twenty others waiting on us to arrive before they could start parachute training. There was also another group of thirty who were halfway through it and would make their jumps a couple of weeks later. Each group was known as a 'promo' and to the rest of the Regiment as the 'black socks brigade'. We hadn't been issued with sports socks yet and our black socks stood out a mile.

We were more or less in isolation from the rest of the camp, not being permitted to leave our building without an escort. We even ran to and from the mess to eat in two columns. In fact, we never walked anywhere, everything was done at a jog and our overall fitness was being raised to another level. We were now running a minimum of 15 kilometres every day. We were taught to fall and roll from ever increasing heights until we progressed to the jump tower in the third week. This was an electric pylon sort of structure with a platform 30 metres off the ground. We were strapped into a parachute harness which was in turn attached to a cable which went up to another platform where your rate of descent was controlled by an instructor on the cable break. As the third week went on so the speed of our descent was increased, and on occasions it felt as if there was no one operating the break. As a result some of our landings were pretty hard which was in no doubt intended to gave us a taste of what the real thing would be like.

At the end of each week we had to complete an 8-kilometre run in full combat kit, 15kg sack (which was weighed), plus your rifle, in under an hour. This was preceded by a 1,500-metre fast run in the same kit which had to be completed in under ten minutes. We then had a five-minute breather before the start of the 8km run.

At first we did well to get round within the given time but as fitness levels rose the times dropped until we were doing the main run in around the 45-minute mark. As part of these tests we had to pick up a sack filled with 80kg of sand and run 60 metres with it slung over your shoulder in under twenty seconds. This simulated carrying someone off the battlefield. We also had to be able to run in sports kit for twelve minutes, covering the maximum distance possible but not less than 2 kilometres. Points were awarded for the distance covered. Failure at any one of these tests meant immediate failure resulting in being returned to Aubagne for reassignment to another regiment. We had already lost six of our group by the end of the second week. Before heading to the mess for any of our meals we had to do six tractions, or pull-ups as they are sometimes known; we then had to do the same thing when we got back.

At last the big week came and we were faced with the final test: the jumps. To gain your jump wings in France you have to make a minimum of six jumps. We were scheduled to make ten including a night jump. That does not sound like a lot but that was only the total number of jumps taken during the promo. Throughout any given year we were expected to make some jumps every time a suitable aircraft paid a visit.

Every two weeks a military transport aircraft equipped for parachuting visited the Regiment for four days of jumping. The airport at Calvi is less than 5 kilometres from the camp and the turn-round time for the aircraft between jumps is only thirty minutes. This meant an enormous number of jumps could be made by the Regiment over the four days. The drop zone was within the perimeter of the camp itself and during 'jump week' the activities of the Regiment revolved around the aim of getting as many jumps in by as many people as possible.

The aircraft would be in the air from first light to dusk, with a two-hour midday break for the flight crew. That meant being ready to leave for the airport at six in the morning, with the last jump around eight in the evening. It was a long day, but we were a parachute regiment and were better paid than the rest of the Army.

The aircraft normally used was the C130 Transall made by France and Germany, and powered by Rolls Royce engines. It was similar to the Hercules but had the advantage of the landing wheels being housed in pods on the outside of the fuselage, unlike the Herc where the wheel bays encroach on the cabin space. It could also fly slower than the Herc, and having only two engines meant there was a lot less turbulence when exiting the aircraft.

Our big day had arrived and we set off at about 7.30 am for the airport – no lorry for us, just a gentle 5kg jog to warm us up. As it was, we arrived at the embarkation site long before anyone else. The vehicle with the parachutes had not even arrived, in fact no one else had and we had to jump over the gate to get in. We had been up since 5.00 and it seemed as if half the day had passed already. The adrenaline was working overtime and I was really excited and nervous at the prospect of making my first jump.

We were looking out to sea watching for the first sight of the plane, but what came out of the bright-blue sky was not what any of us had expected. It looked like a museum piece and it wasn't until it landed and taxied up to where we were waiting that we realized this was the aircraft we would be jumping from. It was a 1950s Nord Atlas – a cigar with wings and two booms trailing back to the rear tail plane. It had radial engines like a Dakota which I thought it was when I first spotted the trails of black smoke when it was still about 5 miles out to sea.

The aircraft made its approach to the airport round the mountains before landing, with the sound of its engines echoing off the hillsides. When I looked at my friends they were all staring at it with their mouths open in disbelief. It was bad enough making our first jump, but from this thing?

The aircraft creaked to a halt about 20 yards from us; close up it looked much larger. What happened next was even more of a surprise – they took the back of the cigar-shaped fuselage off leaving a gaping hole which looked like a cutaway section on a display model. Two loading ramps, like the ones you attach to the back of a trailer to load a car, were attached to the rear of the plane ready for loading.

Suddenly we were on our feet, and collecting our gear from the lorry helped to take our minds off what was to come. We were thrown our main parachute and the reserve from the back of the lorry and made our way back to the embarkation area to put them on. We were in two lines of ten and it only took us a couple of minutes to put the chutes on. This was the moment we had been training for over the past three and a half weeks and the inspection by our instructors went well. The straps between our legs were pulled a bit tighter than was perhaps required, but it would be a brave lad who complained.

When the engines started again the noise was deafening and I was surprised at the heat and force of the exhausts as we were led forward to board the aircraft. We entered by the ramps at the rear, waddling forward like ducks going to a pond. Suddenly everything was much smaller again and the thing that struck me was the absence of seats. The first man in each column was led to the front of the cabin space where he turned round to face the rear and sat down on the floor, with his legs spread as open as he could get them. The next in line did the same and so on until we were all seated in our two lines facing the open hole at the back of the fuselage. The last one seated was only six feet from . . . nothing. The jump master explained that one of the free-fall units would be jumping first, hence the reason for the back of the plane being removed. We would be going out of the side doors as we had been trained. Thank goodness for that.

Once everyone was on board, the aircraft started to taxi to the holding point ready for take-off. Being a qualified pilot none of this took me by surprise, but the noise of the engines as the pilot went through his checks was almost unbearable and we had to put our hands over our ears to protect them.

The disturbing thing was that that meant we had to let go of whatever we had got hold of because of the feeling that we would slide out of the back of the plane as it took off. The sense of speed as we accelerated down the runway was incredible, and the sight of the twin booms flexing up and down didn't add to our feeling of well-being. Within minutes we had climbed out over the coast, the ribbon of golden sand that extended round the entire length of the bay quickly giving way to the beautiful ultramarine waters of the Gulf of Calvi. As we gained height my initial trepidation gave way to a new rush of adrenaline as I took in the magnificent view that was unfolding below me. I was used to flying but this was different, not having anything between us and the ground.

The Nord Atlas climbed slowly in a wide circle and as we gained altitude the drop in air temperature was noticeable. We were climbing to the free-fall drop height of 5,000 feet and it was the end of November. At this time of year even the Med is cold at this altitude. The free-fall team were now standing up and checking each other's gear in preparation for the jump. There was no fuss as they performed the task as if they did this every day, which they practically did.

The aircraft levelled out and was now flying in a straight line towards the drop zone. The jump master was standing at one of the open side doors looking out and forward as he judged the exact position of the plane. At his signal the free-fall team moved as one towards the rear opening. A green light came on and a horn sounded. Before any of us realized what was happening they had taken the final step forward and were gone from our sight below the level of the aircraft. It all happened so quickly and without fuss. I was impressed.

It seemed to take ages for the Nord to descend to our jump height of approximately 1,000 feet, but by this time we were thinking about other things. We stood up, hooked up as we had been taught and waited as our instructors made a final inspection. When the red light came on the first in each line was taken to stand in the door, where he put a hand on each side of the door frame waiting for the order to jump. The instructor at each one had a firm hold of the man's belt as they waited for the light to turn green. I was third in line and could see the beach and the bathers as we rapidly approached the drop zone.

Everything happened so quickly and I must confess that I have little recollection of what happened next. Before I knew it I was out of the door and being jolted back to reality by my chute opening. I looked at the inflated canopy and was relieved to see that everything appeared to be as it should be.

Phew! Looking round me I could see my fellow trainees were all descending safely towards the ground. Because it was our first jump we had exited the aircraft quite slowly and there was a safe distance between us. I was dangling there in my harness enjoying the view and the new sensation of gliding gently along when I suddenly became aware that the ground was now rushing towards me at what seemed an alarming speed.

I did my best to get into the correct position for landing – knees together, legs bent, elbows and chin tucked in. Boom, a quick roll and I was on my knees pulling the lowest parachute cord to deflate my chute which was beginning to billow gently in the slight breeze. I took off my harness as instructed, and wound it in a figure of eight movement round my arms, a bit like winding wool, pushed it into the main parachute sack, threw it over my shoulder and jogged back to the assembly point.

Once we were sure that we had everything packed as it should be, we stood in line in the same order we had jumped. A ground controller then counted us in to make sure that no one was missing and that none of us had any injuries.

I had completed my first jump successfully and it had all happened so quickly that I did not have time to reflect on whether I had been nervous or not, although I knew that I must have been. We were told that this was normal and that it wouldn't be until the third or fourth jump that we would start to question if this was what we really wanted to do.

We took the used chutes to the parachute store where they would be checked for damage before being repacked for reuse. This work was carried out by legionnaires, as is everything else in the Regiment, other than a few female regular army staff who do the machine repairs and are seconded to the regiment. Most have married legionnaires and have been with the Regiment longer than most of the legionnaires. Even so, they wear the red beret of the Regular Army and are not actually part of the Regiment.

Within half an hour we were back at the airport collecting another parachute for the next jump. The aircraft had made several sorties since our first jump and it would be like this all day. By 10.00 am we had completed the second jump and it was planned that we would make a third one in the afternoon. Everyone was full of chat, excited by the morning's activities, all wanting to tell of their own experiences and how easy it had been for them. Time would tell.

We ate a hearty lunch and were back raring to go for our third jump. Although the adrenaline was still doing its thing, I was aware that my mental approach had changed slightly and I was thinking more about what I was about to do.

By 3.00 in the afternoon, we were getting kitted out for the jump. Whether by circumstance or by intention, we were kept hanging about for most of the afternoon while other members of the Regiment made their jumps. The sequence of activity did not let up all afternoon, but hanging around was making some of the lads nervous.

It was starting to get dark quickly and I didn't think we were going to jump again that day when suddenly we found ourselves on the plane, taking off, hooked up and standing in the doorway. The back of the aircraft had been put back on so it was a lot quieter and, on the whole, a lot less stressful. All the same, one of the lads was showing the strain, so the instructor unhooked him from his place in the stick and took him forward to stand in the door so that he would be first out. All went well, the parachutes were handed in and we were off for another well-earned meal.

That evening our instructors debriefed us on how we all felt after the first day's jumping. They were trying to assess if any of us had any doubts about continuing. No one wanted to admit it, but I think that some were having second thoughts. Tomorrow was another day and what we needed now was a good night's sleep. The activities of the day had left us both physically and mentally exhausted.

Morning seemed to come thirty seconds after I had put my head on the pillow, so I must have slept well. After a good breakfast and the statutory pull-ups, we were on our way back to the airport for another long day's jumping. The first jump of the day was an important one as we had to use our chest-mounted reserve parachutes for the first time. It is essential that everyone knows how to deploy the reserve chute in an emergency.

We were lined up in the two sticks, parachutes on, waiting to board the aircraft, when one of the lads stepped forward and said that he couldn't do it. There was no shouting or bullying by the instructors. He was asked if he was sure and, on his confirmation, was removed from the line as we walked forward to board the aircraft. We never saw him again and by the time we got back to our quarters at lunchtime, his locker was empty. He was the first but he wouldn't be the last.

The morning jump with the reserve chute went well. By the time we had cleared the aircraft and I had checked that my principle chute had deployed correctly, it was time to deploy the reserve. This is a lot easier said than done. I pulled the release handle remembering to keep my other hand firmly on the front of the chute to keep it in place. The danger is that the chute falls out and passes between your legs as it fills with air, which would cause you to flip head down with disastrous results. You also have to remember to hold on to the release handle and to stuff it into a pocket. Apart from the obvious danger of it hitting someone on the ground, you would be out on the drop zone until you found it.

Having stuffed the handle into a trouser pocket I took the reserve chute in both hands and threw it as far as I could outwards and downwind like you would a rugby ball. It began to drop slightly but as I waved the cords up and down the chute began to fill and rise in front of me. The descent under two inflated chutes is much slower than it is with one and I made a gentle landing. I had to force myself to roll over as instructed, although there was a great temptation to make a stand-up landing. This would have been noted by the instructors and would result in a punishment of some kind.

Up until now we had made all our jumps without carrying any extra equipment. Such jumps are known in the military parachute world as 'tourist' jumps. The next jump that afternoon would be with everything we would carry into combat. This changes everything as suddenly you have to cope with the extra weight of your pack, weapon and ammunition. The main chute weighs 12kg, the reserve 6kg, your pack a minimum of 15, plus your weapon. All up you are carrying something like 60kg, at least two thirds of your body weight. When you land all of this has to be carried off the drop zone at the double. It was winter and I was sweating just thinking about it.

The pace of jumping was kept up by ourselves and the Regiment as a whole over the four days. By the time our last jump of the promo arrived our numbers had been further reduced. One lad refused to board the aircraft and another would not go to the airport for the last jump.

Our tenth and final jump was scheduled for first thing on the Friday morning – if everything went according to plan we would get our jump wings and be part of the Regiment by the afternoon.

I found myself last in the stick and on the way out of the aircraft one lad hesitated in the door. The delay of those few seconds meant that by the time I left the aircraft we were over the end of the designated drop zone. It was obvious to me when I looked down at the smoke flare on the ground that the wind was going to take me well out of the drop zone. Looking around me I couldn't see any flat areas and the ground seemed to be covered in large boulders and dry-stone dykes. My luck had just run out and I was in for a heavy landing.

I made sure that my landing position was as good as it could be with everything tucked in tight. My pack was still attached to my front and so I released it when I was still 50 to 60 feet off the ground. The pack then hung 10 feet below me on its cord and was the first thing to touch the ground. Three seconds later it was my turn – just before I hit the ground my pack caught on a wall causing me to land at an angle. My left shin bone struck the top of the wall hard enough to dislodge one of the stones. It hurt but after a couple of minutes I was on my feet, gathered up my gear and made my way back to the assembly area. My ankle was sore but I was able to walk rather than run.

About half an hour after we had returned to our room to prepare for the afternoon ceremony, my ankle began to swell, got very sore and extremely hot. I had no option but to report my injury. The camp had its own hospital and medical staff, so after a couple of prodding fingers and an x-ray, I was heading for the plaster room. The outer shin bone of my left ankle had a hairline fracture and a little bit of bone had been chipped off.

The ceremony took place as scheduled that afternoon without me, but I was delighted and surprised when the Colonel in Chief came to the hospital and presented me with my wings. I had made it into the REP at the grand old age of thirty-eight, and I was proud.

CHAPTER 6

La Première Compagnie

We had been told that the Regiment would be going to Tchad in Africa in January for six months. No one wanted to be left behind in Calvi, including me.

Colonel Gadaffi of Libya was flexing his muscles again and had his eyes firmly fixed on taking possession of the northernmost part of Tchad above the sixteenth parallel. The main reason for this was that this mountainous region, known as Tibesti, was rich in uranium. If it was not to give himself the capacity to build an atomic bomb, the value of the uranium to rogue states wishing to do so was way beyond Libya's wildest dreams.

Tchad was a former French colony and still had a military protection treaty with France. This ensured that there was always a large French military presence with over 10,000 army and air force personnel on Tchadian soil at any one time. There had been a steady increase in the number of Libyan incursions into Tchadian territory over the past couple of months resulting in Tchad asking for France to step up its military assistance.

Meanwhile, back in Calvi, I was getting used to moving about on crutches. Once more I was being told that due to a combination of my injury and age, I would probably be assigned to administrative duties. I didn't mind that but I would be disappointed if the Regiment left for Tchad without me. However, luckily for me, the combat companies were being expanded from three to four operational sections each. Our promo was the last before the Regiment would deploy in January and the first company required every last one of us to take them up to full combat strength. Each section comprised a commanding officer (normally a Lieutenant), a second in command (Sergeant Chef) and four combat groups made up of a Sergeant or Caporal Chef, a Caporal and eight men in each group. That was an additional thirty-eight men per company.

It was up to the company commanding officer to make the final selection and I had to present myself to him on my crutches. Normally I wouldn't have held out much hope but I had forgotten that this was the Legion and normal is not a word used very often. I liked him immediately but he made it quite clear to me that if my ankle was still in plaster by Christmas Day, I wouldn't be going anywhere. These were his exact words: 'still in plaster'.

*

On 1 December, the doctor told me that the cast would have to stay on for at least another thirty days. As the Regiment would be departing on 15 January, time was not on my side. In the meantime I was assigned to the fourth group of the fourth section. My new section was to be made up of a mix of old and new. We had a new Lieutenant straight out of Saint Cyr, the elite officers' academy just outside Paris – the French equivalent of Sandhurst. The senior NCO was a Scot who had had a very colourful background to say the least, if everything said about him was true. He had been up and down the ranks a couple of times and was now a Sergeant Chef. He was very experienced and respected by everyone from the Colonel down. The sergeants had come through the ranks and had always been in the Regiment. Our caporals were more of a mixed bunch. One was Irish and would become a close friend, one was French and a bit of a head banger, one was a Belgian and I never did find out where the fourth one came from. He was a strange guy to say the least and kept himself to himself.

We were all given a particular function within each group: radio operator, medic, sniper, light-machine gunner and two riflemen – at least, that was the theory. My shooting results during basic training had been good and due to the lack of time to send any of us on a specialist course, training would be given on the job. It was decided that I would fill the roll of sniper and I was issued with a FRF 1, 7.62mm, standard-issue sniper's rifle, complete with telescopic sight and an image intensifier for firing in the dark. It was all very impressive if I could get fit in time. Between 5 December and the first week in January I fired an average of fifty rounds a day at distances up to 800 metres in daylight, and at 400 metres at night. I got to know my rifle quite well.

Christmas was approaching fast and I was only too aware that the deadline for getting out of my plaster cast was too. The doctor and my Captain were sticking to their respective dates and it wasn't looking good.

Christmas is a big thing in the Legion and the preparations were well under way. Each section in every company set up a bar and decorated it with a theme. Being a Roman Catholic country, the companies each built a religious crèche which again had to have a theme telling a story with a taped message. Each crèche was judged for its originality, construction and theme, with a prize going to the winning one and a trophy that was kept by the company for the year. It was very competitive and a great deal of time and effort went into their manufacture.

The end results would have put a Harrods Christmas window to shame. A panel comprising senior officers and local dignitaries visited each crèche on the afternoon of the 24th and the result was announced just after midnight. The camp was open to the public on the afternoon of Christmas

Day and the locals came in their hundreds to see them. It's a very French thing but nice all the same to see how hard everyone worked and the pride they took in the end product. You didn't have to be religious to enjoy taking part – it was all part of that special bond that is almost unique to the Legion.

I was learning that a major part of the Legion philosophy was that every Legionnaire should feel a member of the large family that is the Legion. A mass was held on Christmas Eve for those who wished to attend and included the wives, partners and children of those who were of Caporal Chef rank and above. By nine in the evening all family members had to leave the camp and all military personnel spent the evening with their respective companies. We ate a collective meal and members of each company would put on the entertainment. It was amazing the range of hidden talent within the ranks – from classical pianists to good guitar players, singers and comedians. It was the only time when the 'other ranks' could take the mickey out of the officers.

After the meal we all retired to our respective bars before 'doing the rounds'. Our Captain was due to address the Company just after midnight and I was still in plaster. Drastic situations demand drastic measures. The doctor had said that he wouldn't take the cast off before the thirty days had passed and my Captain had said, 'If you're still in plaster, you won't be going anywhere. So I went to my room and set about it with a knife. It was a lot harder to cut through than I thought that it would be, but after half an hour of hard graft I was 'cast free'. I put on as tight a strapping as I could, bearing in mind I had to get my shoe on. I then got back into my dress uniform and went to the main room in time for the Captain's address.

My ankle was very stiff, but at least it wasn't particularly painful. My Lieutenant noticed immediately and called me over with a wave of his finger. All he said was, 'I won't ask, so don't tell me. I don't want to know, but the Captain will.'

After the Captain's address and he had wished us all a Happy Christmas, he called me over. There was no point in lying about what I had done, so in my basic French I told him what I had done, and my reasoning. When I had finished he said that he would delay any decision until I had seen the doctor – it was up to him to declare me fit or not. So far so good.

The evening went well and I sat as much as possible to keep the weight off my ankle, but it was inevitable that I would bump into the doctor sooner or later. He took one look at me, wished me 'A merry Christmas and be in my surgery first thing Monday morning,' shook my hand and walked away. I enjoyed the rest of the evening and was able to rest up for most of Christmas Day.

At eight o'clock on the Monday morning I was seated in the waiting room at the hospital. The doctor held the rank of Colonel and therefore I was dressed in full dress uniform. An hour later I was called into his consulting room. I did my best to explain my position, bearing in mind my limited command of the French language. He didn't even examine me but ordered me out to run four laps of the 400-metre running track. He had a clear view from his window so I had no way of cheating. Normally the distance was nothing but I was in full uniform complete with kepi, and I suffered. It was painful and I was very hot, but despite that I kept up a good pace round the track. It was no use hobbling round as I had to persuade him that I was fit. I was soon back in his consulting room and he asked me if I had had any problems.

The sweat was pouring off me but I said no. He looked at me for ages before he spoke. 'On your own head be it,' then he signed me off as fit for operations. No light duties, no recuperation time, just get on with it.

I was greatly relieved even if I knew that it was not going to be easy. When I reported back to the Company the Captain had already spoken to the doctor on the phone. The Company was due to leave for Tchad in two weeks and he made it clear that I had until then to prove my fitness or he would leave me behind.

There was much to do in preparation for our pending departure and little time for physical activities. I found that I was able to jog at a reasonable pace for relatively short distances and always made sure that I was up with the rest at the end of each run. I was aware that the pace was not being pushed to enable me to keep up. It was another demonstration of the solidarity and team spirit that exists within the Legion.

The first few days were difficult but the pain in my ankle began to ease and I kept it well strapped to give it extra support. With the preparations completed we were given a week's embarkation leave in Calvi. This was the first real break I had had since joining and I hadn't even been into town. The weather was beautiful and it gave me a chance to recover while relaxing. Calvi was beautiful, and along with my friends we explored every bar and restaurant. We sat out on the terraces and soaked up the winter sun – just what the doctor ordered in more ways than one.

On 15 January 1984, we flew out of Calvi to the French air base of Istre on the Mediterranean coast, just west of Marseille. After a two-hour stopover we embarked on two transport command DC8s for Tchad. I had not appreciated the great distances involved when travelling in Africa. I knew it was big, but not that big.

We flew over Corsica and down the east coast of Sardinia towards Sicily.

We then crossed over to Malta before heading south into Egyptian air space to give me my first look at the great African continent. We were flying at 25,000 feet, the sky was crystal clear and the sand of the desert spread out below us as far as we could see. The great dunes looked like the ripples of sand on a beach after the tide goes out. I knew from that very moment that I was about to experience something special.

The flight took over four hours on a flight path that took us over the great city of Cairo before following the River Nile southwards. Somewhere over the Egyptian frontier with the Sudan we turned south-west on a direct heading for Tchad. As we passed over the Darfur mountains the aircraft began its descent towards the Tchadien capital, Ndjamena.

When we had left in mid-afternoon it had been about 6°C (42°F); it was now dark and when we finally came to a halt, and the doors of the aircraft were opened, the heat hit us like a brick wall. It was late evening local time and 22°C (74°F). We were in Africa.

After leaving the aircraft we had to pass through passport control. Officially I was now French, or at least that's what the passport said, but we didn't actually have to present them as we passed in front of the Tchadian official. He just welcomed us to his country with a nod. We then returned to the tarmac and began unloading the tons of freight we had brought with us on the aircraft.

By the time we had finished it was 11.00 pm local time, and we were all tired and soaked to the skin with sweat. After we had eaten we were taken to a hangar where rows of camp beds were laid out. We had been up since 5.00 am and couldn't care less where we put our heads down. They kept the hangar doors open to let in what little air there was but it was still stifling hot and the only godsend was that it was not yet the time of year for mosquitoes. I, like everyone else, was sound asleep within minutes of lying down.

By 6.00 am we were up, had been fed, the beds had been put away and we were on lorries heading for what would be our base camp for the next four weeks. The road followed the great river Chari as we headed towards the outskirts of the capital. It was only a short ten-minute trip to the camp which looked out across the river which formed the frontier between Tchad and Cameroon.

After settling into our new accommodation blocks, we were briefed on what our duties were, how we should behave to the local population and what the 'rules of engagement' were. This was a country where 'Black Africa met Arab Africa', which was part of the problem.

Our first priority was the protection of France's interests, to ensure the safety of the European and American residents and to assist the maintenance of law and order within the country. We would assist the Tchadian military to secure the frontiers of the country against any invasion, but we were not there to keep the existing government in power against the democratic wishes of the people.

For most of the month we patrolled deeper and deeper into the desert without sight nor sound of any enemy. We soon became used to the dry heat of the day and the low temperatures at night. The sand gave up its heat quickly once the sun went down and woollen sweaters had to be worn in the evening. I had fallen in love with the desert – it was so clean and at first glance untouched by man. Nothing was left to waste, every last scrap being used by the few inhabitants who lived in this hostile and at times life threatening environment.

Everything about the desert was impressive, particularly the size, the emptiness and the silence. At night there was no light pollution from towns or industry to obscure the night sky, which was filled with millions of stars – you could even watch the passage of satellites with the naked eye. I had never seen anything so amazing and it made me realize just how small mankind was. We were like one of the grains of sand in the desert we were standing in, such was the scale of things.

Two days after we returned to the capital we were put on two hours' standby, twenty-four hours a day. Word was coming in that a French Mirage reconnaissance fighter with a crew of two had been shot down deep inside Tchadian territory. We were immediately briefed to perform a search and rescue mission and to drive out the Libyan patrol that was suspected of being guilty of the attack. The incident had taken place in north-western Tchad, somewhere along the 16th parallel which traversed the country. To give an idea of the distances involved, if we set out overland, and assuming the enemy stayed where they were, it would take us three weeks to cross the desert to get there.

Within an hour and a half of the alert we were airborne in a Transall heading for the town of Moussorro where there was a French forward air base. Even this was two hours' flying time from the capital. From there it was planned that we would transfer to Puma helicopters for the rest of the mission. It was assumed by everyone that we would press on immediately in the hope of recovering the crew quickly. We didn't know the status of the pilots and a quick recovery was essential as they could be under attack on the ground from the Libyan patrol.

To our surprise we were put on hold while the logistics for the operation were put in place. The distances were so great that the helicopters would need to refuel out in the desert to be able to complete the mission. Tankers with a ground escort were already heading out to the rendezvous point, but it would take them a day at least to get there, which meant that the helicopters were going nowhere until they knew that they could be refueled. It also gave the diplomats time to try to defuse the situation, if only for the sake of the stranded pilots. We were told that they had ejected and that they were close to the downed aircraft. At least we had an exact location for the operation and would not have to search for them.

Hours turned into two days before we were given the go-ahead, which must have given the attacking group plenty of time to get clear of the area. But ours was not to reason why, just to get on with it. The tankers were in place having being escorted across the desert by the 1ere REC, the Legion tank regiment whose home base was in Orange, just north of Avignon in southern France. They were equipped with six-wheeled armoured vehicles called RC10s, which were ideal for the sand. They had the ability to move over all types of terrain at high speed while having the firepower of a main battle tank with their 120mm guns.

When we eventually took off, the four Pumas were escorted by two Gazelle helicopter gunships and there would be additional fighter cover in the area if required. As we neared the downed aircraft the Gazelles reported that there was no sign of the Libyans. They were long gone. We landed within a couple of hundred metres of the wreckage as we could not be sure that the Libyans had not left behind surprise presents such as mines, before withdrawing.

From the tracks left in the sand it appeared that the attacking force had been made up of half a dozen 4x4 vehicles, probably Toyota Landcruiser pick-ups, which were the preferred form of transport in this part of the world, with 20mm anti-aircraft guns mounted on the back. The soldiers would have been armed with Russian or Chinese AK47 assault rifles and RPG7 shoulder-fired rockets. The rockets were simple but effective against soft-skinned vehicles but were of little use against armour. There are lots of more sophisticated weapons on the market, but you should never forget that it doesn't matter a damn what kind of weapon kills you, you are dead and that's that.

There were no mines round the wreckage and we were clear to make our approach. It was clear that the crew had not survived the crash. The cockpit canopy was still in place and their bodies were strapped to their seats. The risk to us was that the ejector seats might be unstable. The aircraft was extensively damaged by the crash and there was evidence of it having been hit by a rocket. I think that they must have come in low for a closer look and a lucky shot with an RPG had brought it down. There had been no fire and the aircraft's weapons were still in place, except for one missile which was found a short distance from the crash site. We had brought an expert with us and it took an hour before he was sure that it was safe to remove the bodies.

We took photographs of the crash site and removed the two flight recorders. Further examination of the wreckage revealed multiple bullet holes which had penetrated the engine. We therefore took more photographs which could be used by the crash investigators. Nothing else could be salvaged so it was decided to destroy the aircraft with explosives. After the charges had been detonated we flew back low over the crash site. There was nothing left that would not be covered by the next sandstorm and that looked like being sooner than we had thought.

The wind was beginning to rise and the sky had turned a greyish brown colour to the south, the direction we had to go to reach our refueling point. The pilots were keen to be on their way, but we were not even half an hour into the journey before the decision was made to land. By now there was a wall of sand towering into the sky across the whole of the horizon. The air intakes of the helicopter engines were covered and ropes tied to the rotor blades. Each rope was then tied round the waist of a Legionnaire who lay down in the sand with his back to the wind to wait the arrival of the storm.

We all had the traditional headgear worn by the nomads, called a 'sech'. This was a yard-long piece of fine woven cloth that you wrapped round your head like a turban. When the wind and sand got up you covered your mouth and ears with it to keep out the sand. The fine weave acted as a barrier but let you breath. We also had sand goggles although you couldn't even see your hand when you held it up in front of your face.

The temperature had risen dramatically and was now well into the mid-40s (120°F). It was difficult to breath and the sand was building up at my back like a snowdrift protecting me from the force of the wind. It was not a pleasant experience.

The worst of the storm passed over us within half an hour but we had to wait another couple of hours until the sand in the air had settled enough to let us take the covers off the engines. The finer particles of sand, which were suspended in the air, would have clogged the engines in seconds. We just had to be patient, something every soldier needs to be. There is a military saying: 'Hurry up and wait'.

The remainder of the journey back to base was uneventful but it took us several hours to clean all our equipment. A blocked rifle caused by a man not taking the time to clean it properly could cost him his life. We had all found another use for one of man's greatest inventions, the condom – you simply slipped it over the barrel of your rifle and kept it in place with an elastic band. It kept everything out just as efficiently as it kept everything in. If you had to use it in a hurry you didn't even have to take it off unless you were firing blanks – no pun intended.

Our next deployment took us to the north-eastern part of the country where we occupied an old fort at the small town of Iriba, which was a meeting point for the camel trains which still cross the Sahara. There was a good, deep, freshwater well on the outskirts of the town which was the sole reason for the town's existence. The entrance to the fort had been built at the turn of the century from red brick. I have no idea where the bricks came from as there was nothing like it for hundreds of miles. I can only assume that every last brick had been brought in on the back of a camel.

There was a desert landing strip about 5 miles out of the town which was used to fly in supplies for the base. This was the only direct link with the outside world – it took at least a month to get there overland. There were no roads as we know them, only mile after mile of sand with not a single feature to guide you. All navigation out here was done by the sun, the stars and today with the aid of a good GPS system. Such a thing was unheard of in 1984 and a compass was the only technical aid we could rely on. The airstrip was no more than half a mile of flat sand, there were no buildings and the only landing aids were tins of oil that we lit if visibility was poor. Night landings were for emergencies only. It was a strange part of the country with pyramid-style hills dotted about the landscape several miles apart. The nearest one to the landing strip was about half a mile away and about 900 feet high; it dominated the landscape with commanding views in all directions. An observation post was established on the top and was manned day and night. We made shelters from the sun with tarpaulins stretched between the rocks, then dusted them with sand to camouflage the site. Each group did a week's guard duty, but it was very hot, cramped and boring.

Very little happened in the area and we organized lizard races to keep ourselves amused. The greatest danger was sunburn and dehydration, and we had to have water brought out to us every day as it was important to keep up our fluid intake. A couple of the lads had to descend to the foot of the hill every morning to collect the supplies and it was no joke climbing back up in the heat. We always tried to do it while the sun cast a shadow over that side of the hill.

The problem being in such temperatures is that the more you drink, the more you sweat, and the more you drink. It is important to try and keep your body temperature as close to that of the ambient temperature – which was why the locals drank so much hot tea. The temptation was to drink cold liquids but that only made us feel worse.

One afternoon a troupe of baboons appeared at the foot of the hill. There were about a dozen of them and they were being led by the Alpha male in a single column. When they came to a bit of open ground they wanted to cross, the troupe formed a line at the edge of the clearing under relative cover while the 'boss' dashed across the gap to the other side. Once over he had a look around before calling for the rest to follow. They dashed over in a line abreast before reforming in their column to continue their journey. Perfect military tactics.

It was still important to clean our weapons constantly, which also gave us something else to do. We were all tired having been there for five days, but it had to be done. One of the group was cleaning his side arm, and had just reassembled it and put the 9mm ammunition clip back on. Quite how he did it I don't know, but he fired a round. He was left handed and somehow or other he had the barrel pointing at his left wrist when it went off. He was about to get jumped all over by our sergeant when he saw that he was just sitting there in a state of shock staring at his wrist. We gave him first aid and stopped the bleeding before calling in a helicopter to lift him off the hill back to the fort. It would be morning before he was airlifted to Ndjamina for hospital treatment. He had been lucky and the bullet had passed through his wrist without touching bone or artery. Luckier still, no one else had been injured, considering that he had been sitting in the middle of a group of six.

When not on the hill, we went on long-range patrols along the camel train routes. On the whole the nomads were friendly people who were always willing to share what little they had with us. They had no loyalties to any particular government and recognized no frontiers. They sought no assistance but were willing to trade for anything that took their fancy. Theirs was a unique combination of worldly experience and innocence. What was happening in the big bad world was of no consequence to them and I envied them their way of life. It was harsh but made you realize that happiness is not something that you can buy. Equality of the sexes is not something known in these parts – all the physical work is done by the women while the men sit around and chat. Even at the well it was the women who were doing all the hard work.

The well was deep and a donkey was used to haul the water up in a container made out of goat skin. As much water seemed to leak out as was being brought up, but at least it fell back down the well so it wasn't lost. Before we left the fort we were able to rig them up a more efficient system. The women expressed their gratitude but the men couldn't see the point. As far as they were concerned, water had been drawn up this way for hundreds of years, so why change now? Perhaps they had a point. When our contraption wore out they would go back to using goat skins anyway.

When our time at the fort was over we were replaced by another section from our company. We headed south overland to the town of Abéché, a town I would visit many times over the coming years. Again we occupied an old army camp that had seen better days. The camp itself was on the road to the airport, which was home to a larger French Air Force detachment. This one had a tarmac runway and was used as a forward base for a couple of French fighters and as a freight depot. Regular French Army units were also stationed in the town but they were housed in Portakabins complete with air-conditioning.

We didn't even have electricity, but the Legion isn't the Legion for nothing and before the first week was out we had begged, borrowed or stolen most of what we needed to make life more comfortable. Most of our time was spent out on patrol anyway, but that didn't mean that we had to slum it.

Sanitation was a big problem and most of us suffered from one stomach problem or another while we were there. No one was exempt. We had dug latrines a couple of hundred yards downwind from our quarters. Two hundred yards is a long way when you are in a hurry, so we managed to spirit up a couple of old bicycles out of nowhere to speed up the journey. Even then some didn't quite make it and there was a lot of cursing when the bikes hadn't been returned to the correct place. Despite this we had an easier time there than we had had during the previous month.

While in Abéché we met some French nuns from a little convent which had been in existence since the Second World War. They were living on the edge of poverty and to this day the Regiment sends them help in the form of clothes and books for the little orphanage they run in the town.

Abéché is on the frontier with Darfur and has more recently been overrun by refugees from the Sudan crisis. These sisters had been forgotten by their Church and I am sure that they are still working there helping the refugees without any outside help. The 'big' charities spend millions on promoting themselves and little else, while there are hundreds of small groups like the sisters in Abéché who just get on with it and get no recognition or thanks for their dedication.

Tchad is a predominantly Muslim country in the grip of war and poverty, but the Catholic Church has seen fit to spend hundreds of thousands of pounds building an enormous cathedral in the capital which can seat 5,000. It mostly serves the small European and foreign diplomatic communities which at best will see a hundred or so attending Mass on a Sunday. Don't get me wrong, the other Christian Churches and charities are no better. If the people at home saw what really happens to the money or goods they give for the 'wider work of the Church', or other big-name charities, they would be horrified. I have seen 4x4s bought with the money donated by children in the

UK being used as military transport with guns and rockets mounted on the back. The 'Blue Peter' symbols still painted on the doors.

We spent the last month of our six-month stay in the south of the country. It was hard to believe that we were in the same country. Desert gave way to lush farmlands in less than 20 miles, but the desert was gaining a few miles every year. Most of the erosion was caused by the indiscriminate cutting of trees and brushwood for fuel – nature did the rest.

The farmlands quickly turn to forest as you approach the frontier with the Central African Republic, another French protectorate. This whole region had been part of the French colonies until just after the Second World War, but were now independent states which maintained military assistance agreements with France.

Tchad is the crossroads for racial, cultural and religious differences in Africa. Arabic and black African cultures meet head on and it was an explosive mix. The black Africans in the south were the administrators and mostly Christian. The Arabs of the north were warriors and mostly Muslim. Neither trusted the other and this was the main cause of the military strife that dominated the region. This is exactly the problem in the Sudan which has led to the catastrophic situation in that war-torn country today. Despite all the best intentions of the UN, there is no real solution to the problem and we in the West are unable to solve it. Our idea of democracy means nothing in this part of the world, yet trying to 'enforce' it is our idea of the solution.

My first six months in Africa were at an end and it was time to head back to Calvi for a well-earned rest. On the whole it had been a good introduction to military life at the blunt end, but I was looking forward to a bit of normality for a while, or at least my stomach was.

CHAPTER 7

Normality, Legion Style

Back in Calvi we set about the routine of cleaning and repairing all our equipment before putting it back in store ready for the next mission. France operates a rapid intervention alert system with selected regiments grouped under the umbrella of 'Force d'Action Rapide', or FAR as it is more commonly known. There is always a regiment on standby for immediate deployment anywhere in the world with each regiment taking it in turn for a month on what is known as G1.

Every Legionnaire has two alert kits in store at all times – one for cold climates and one for hot – ready for immediate deployment. Within the Regiment, during the month on alert, one of the companies is on two-hour standby twenty-four hours a day. The rest of the Regiment is on six-hour standby. This means that the company on two-hour standby must be able to assemble with all its necessary equipment ready for deployment within two hours of the alert being given, with the rest of the Regiment in six.

It sounds simple, but in practice it is a huge logistical problem. When an alert is given, all personnel must be on camp within the hour, whether involved in the alert or not, as everyone has a part to play in helping the standby company get ready. There are regular practice alerts to ensure that the call-out system works. If the alert is sounded out of normal daytime working hours, the camp central telephone switchboard calls selected personnel, who then call everyone on their list. This frees up the switchboard on camp to deal with more urgent communications.

It works well and buses are sent to prearranged pick-up points in town for those who don't have their own transport. These alert practices are normally held at about 2.00 in the morning and by about 7.00 am the whole Regiment is on parade with all their equipment ready for inspection. The operational staff are given an intervention scenario and have to have the planning for the operation completed in time for the first and second deployments, according to the laid-down timescale. The important thing is that no one knows if the alert is an exercise or not, except for the most senior officers. If it is an exercise, stand down doesn't take place until about ten hours into the alert, then everything has to be put back into storage. This can take the rest of the day as all the equipment has to be cleaned and repacked ready for the real thing which could happen five minutes after everything is back to normal.

With everything stored away after our trip to Africa, we were given three weeks' leave. Normally legionnaires with less than a full year's service are not permitted to leave the island, but due to the circumstances we were allowed to take our leave in mainland France, one condition being that we had to stay in France. We didn't have passports anyway which would normally have ensured that this instruction was obeyed.

Apart from the week's leave in Calvi before we left for Tchad, this was my first real rest since joining in Paris in June 1983. I had my military ID card but with no other documents, I could not return to the UK in theory, nor did I have any civilian clothing. Rules are rules, but are there to be flaunted, and my friends and I had no intention of staying in France. We were homeward bound.

We flew from Calvi to Paris on a scheduled flight, but by the time we got into the centre of Paris it was after six in the evening and the shops were starting to close. We had been told by other Brits that the easiest way to get back to the UK was by overnight ferry from Dunkirk to Dover. The train was due to leave at seven which did not give us much time to shop for some civilian clothing. We found a small clothes shop near the station and were able to buy the basics for a quick change.

One of my friends was a Canadian who had family living on the Isle of Man. He rushed into a shoe shop, bought the first pair of shoes he saw in his size, threw them in the box, paid for them and rushed to the station. We made it by the skin of our teeth onto the train and got into an empty compartment. We were all feeling good as we changed into our new civilian clothes, until there was a verbal explosion from the Canadian. In his haste to buy his shoes he had not noticed that he had bought two left shoes. He was so angry with himself that he threw them out of the window, which luckily was open at the time.

When we got to Dunkirk we had about an hour to spare before the ferry sailed at midnight. To our surprise the Police on passport control did not bat an eye when we presented our military ID cards, nor did they ask us for passports. They knew from our build, haircuts and tans exactly who we were and waved us through to board the ship. So far so good.

It was a slow crossing and we slept on the reclining lounge chairs for most of the voyage. We woke early, shaved and had some breakfast before going on deck to watch the ship enter Dover harbour. Now we had to face the next obstacle: UK passport control. The worst that could happen was that we would be sent back.

The ship docked at 6.00 am and we prepared to present ourselves at passport control. I had to admit that we stood out from the crowd. We seemed to be expected and were shown into a side room where we were met by two uniformed police officers and a plain-clothes officer from Special Branch.

It took about half an hour for them to check our identities but there was no other problem and we were allowed to catch the next train to London. They were used to legionnaires coming back into the country via Dover – in fact they preferred it and asked us to pass on the word to any others that this was the way they should come if they did not have their passports.

Before going our separate ways we agreed to meet up in London for the trip back to France. I got the first train to Glasgow and went straight to the passport office to apply for a replacement.

I told them that I had misplaced my existing one, but didn't think that I had lost it and needed an urgent replacement for my work. After waiting a couple of hours I handed over the appropriate fee and was issued with a new one.

During my absence my mother had moved to Aberdeen to be near my brother and his family, so that was where I headed. I had written to her a couple of times from Tchad but had not expected a reply. Despite everything the reunion passed well enough, but I still spent more time at my brother's house with my sister-in-law than I did with my mother.

By the end of the second week I was ready to make the journey back to France. I realized that I had moved on and that I had no real friends here who shared my interests any more. My Legion friends and I met up in London as planned and found that we had all more or less felt the same way, so were happy enough to be heading back to France. We had a couple of fun days together in Paris where we met up with other members of the Regiment and I got to know some of the better non-tourist bars, which over the years have been frequented by legionnaires. They are decorated with photographs and souvenirs supplied by legionnaires passing through Paris and reflected the multi-national, multi-racial unique mix that is the Legion.

We all changed back into uniform at the airport before the flight back to Calvi, which was almost all legionnaires who, although in high spirits, were well behaved and entertained the few civilians on board to a repertoire of Legion songs. These were, after all, young men with enormous energy who need to be doing something out of the ordinary all the time to keep them going.

I wanted to improve my French and to develop management skills, so I put myself forward for a three-month administration course. This was held at the

2eme REI (2nd Foreign Infantry Regiment) in Nimes, France. There was a place available on the course starting in September so I took it.

The 2eme REI was a fully mechanized infantry regiment. At that time it was the first Legion regiment to be equipped with the new light-armoured personnel carriers, which are capable of making an amphibious crossing. Some of the VABs (Vehicule Avant Blinde) were equipped with 20mm automatic cannon which were fired from inside the vehicle. The front armour is heavy enough to withstand machine-gun rounds or a rocket attack. They have four-wheel independent drive and suspension making them faster and more manoeuvrable than an equivalent tracked vehicle. They are not light at just over 11 tons but offer excellent protection for transporting a combat group.

The city of Nimes is famous for two things. The first is its Roman heritage and magnificent coliseum in the centre of the town, where gladiators from the Roman legions would have fought. Its second claim to fame is being the home of the famous Lacoste clothing company.

I enjoyed my three months there and had the company of the Irish Caporal from my group, who was also on the course. I don't know how much I learned but I had a great time. All French military personnel are issued with travel passes which entitle you to a 75 per cent reduction on public transport, including the wonderful high-speed trains that run the length and breadth of the country.

We had every weekend off and as Nimes is well served by the TGV express trains, we could be whipped off to Paris in three hours, and what was more, they ran on time and were spotless. When the timetable says that a train will arrive at a given time and stop for three minutes, that is exactly what it does.

We visited Avignon, Marseille, Paris and all stops north during our stay, and really got to know a lot about this beautiful country – and I was being paid at the same time. The only mishap I had during the course was that I managed to break a finger playing rugby, but apart from that I had a great time.

Before we knew it we were back in Calvi in time for Christmas. I was now the proud holder of my first qualification: a 'Certificate Technique Elimentaire' in administration management. I had been in the Legion for just over a year when I was promoted to 'Legionnaire Première Classe' and was given my first stripe. I received a pay rise for both the qualification and rank, I felt great and had a wonderful Christmas.

As already mentioned, France has several military cooperation treaties with its former colonies. Apart from the opportunity of seeing and working in another part of the world, it paid well. When on an overseas tour we received two and a half times our normal pay, which was very nice for the bank balance as we had nothing to spend it on while on operations. Everything was provided for, including in our off-duty time to keep us entertained. Normally there was nowhere for us to go outside the base, but there were videos in the evenings and mess costs were next to nothing. On top of that, operational patrols let you see the remoter parts of these countries that have no access for tourists – had there been, such visits would have cost a fortune.

In February 1985, the whole Regiment left for the Republic of Central Africa. We were stationed in the north-west of the country at a town called Bouar, about 300 miles from the capital, Bangui. This was equitorial Africa and a complete contrast to the deserts of Tchad.

After a couple of weeks acclimatizing to the heat and humidity, our section was given the task of building a road bridge across a river in the north-west of the country. There had never been a bridge at this particular part of the river and it was only possible to cross it by a ford at certain times of the year. The building of this bridge would open up the economy of the region and had been talked about for years. It was a huge task for us and would take the best part of a month to complete. The site had been surveyed and the plans drawn up by civil engineers, but no one until now had been prepared to take on the job. The location was remote, the climate hostile and the cost of a civilian firm doing the job would have been prohibitive. So here we were – the Legion to the rescue. After all, we could do anything, couldn't we, or so we were told.

Our first task on arriving at the site was to build ourselves a camp. If you are going to be in a fixed location for any length of time you may as well make yourself as comfortable as possible. Life in a hostile environment such as this is a lot easier if you can look forward to good meals and basic home comforts. To this end, we built ourselves a first-class field kitchen, with a wood-fired oven to bake fresh bread in. There was no shortage of fresh meat which we hunted ourselves. The local village had plenty of vegetables in the market and there was a remarkable range of fish in the river – some of them called Captain fish were so large that one fish could feed the whole section.

Our big problem was fresh water. The river itself was the problem as it carried one particular parasite which, if it got under your skin, caused severe sickness and diarrhoea. There was even a ban on washing clothes in the river. As a result, we had to have fresh water brought to us by road tanker. We also set up a water purification system which we would leave behind when we left, to be used by the villagers.

We had our own medical team with us and they set up a clinic which was used by the locals. Word soon got out and they arrived in droves, some walking days to get to the clinic for treatment. This was a 'hearts and minds' operation as was building the bridge. Every morning there was a line of villagers waiting to be seen but when the queue got longer by the day, it became necessary to have the village elders install some kind of order. Some of the ailments we saw were of such a serious nature that they would normally have required hospital treatment. Our doctors did the best they could under the circumstances, but the nearest hospital facilities were in the capital which was over 700 miles away, and there was no real public transport system. As far as we could gather, a doctor visited the area for a few days twice a year, and that was it.

Each village had its own 'medicine man' who made his own potions, which had been used with some success, it must be said, over the centuries. They were not to be mocked and some of the potions worked, but not a lot.

The fame of our cuisine was also spreading and every French military patrol in the area seemed to call in on us at meal times. Our English chef was turning out fresh 'Cornish pasties' and steak pies baked in our bread oven, which had been made out of a large biscuit tin covered in baked earth. He had learned how to get the temperature just right and the results were simply fantastic.

The section worked well together and the central supports of the bridge were quickly built. The concrete set almost as fast as we mixed it and we were soon ready to install the huge steel support beams. There were eight of them and they had to be brought up to us on military tank transporters, each beam weighing in at almost 20 tons. They had also brought a mobile crane to lift them off the transporters, but it couldn't lift them into place. Big problem.

It was now that the weeks of medical co-operation with the local villages were to bear fruit. With the help of the local chiefs we assembled two teams, each of one hundred natives. The beams would have to be carried into place. Getting them to the river's edge meant passing a hundred lengths of rope under them, then, with a hundred men on each side, the natives took the strain on the ropes and lifted the beams off the ground. They started chanting with deep voices as they shuffled forward, directed by their own leaders. This was not slave labour, these men knew that they were helping themselves and were proud to be doing so. As their voices boomed out the first beam was slowly lifted, carried forward and lined up ready to be moved into position. It was a wonderful experience and one that will stay for ever engraved on my memory.

A wooden frame had been constructed to enable the beams to be carried to their final resting places. This was slow, tiring work and it took three days for the eight beams to be carried into place. We then had to lay cross timbers to form the road surface and erect side barriers. This took another three weeks to complete and by the time we had finished the work we felt as if we had constructed the Forth Road Bridge.

To formally open the bridge, our Colonel in Chief flew in by helicopter to cut the ceremonial ribbon. He called the chiefs from the villages nearest to the crossing which had provided most of the labour to join him in performing the opening ceremony. There was much singing and dancing by the villagers as they celebrated an event which would change their lives for ever.

But all good things come to an end, and we had to dismantle our base and our celebrated oven. Within weeks the vegetation would claim back our camp site and there would be no trace of our passage – except for the bridge, of course.

The rest of the Regiment had been busy in our absence and had been building accommodation huts to replace the tents which had been in place when we first arrived in Bouar. They had built shower blocks and a mess area, with recreational facilities such as a large video room, table tennis and an indoor gymnasium. The wet season was approaching which would keep everyone indoors when off duty. The icing on the cake was the magnificent entrance gate which carried the regimental badge and name. There were two other French Regular Army units stationed in the town and they were living under canvas in very basic conditions.

After a couple of weeks of normal duties, we headed south-west into the tropical rainforest close to the frontier with the Congo. Our mission was to escort a routine Gendarmerie border patrol.

For over a hundred miles we drove along a huge tarmac road with no traffic except for the occasional timber lorry. This super highway had started life as the Trans African Highway, paid for by loans from the International Monetary Fund and the World Bank. Like most of these giant projects, once the initial publicity was over and the politicians had had their moment of fame, the money found its way elsewhere, such as their own pockets, and the projects came to a halt.

As the trees got as tall as the road was wide, we came across a road sign for 'road narrows' – and it did. Our six-lane highway dead-ended into a forest track barely wide enough to take our vehicles. From brilliant sunshine we went in to almost total darkness as the tree canopy blocked out the sun. It was hot and the humidity had gone up to 90 per cent. Everything was dripping wet and there was a powerful smell of decaying vegetation. Now and again we would burst into a clearing which was completely carpeted with wild orchids. We had no option but to drive over them as there was no other way to go – an orchid grower would have cried, but there was nothing else we could do.

The highlight of the patrol was meeting the wonderful pygmy people. They came out to greet us and ran alongside singing their strange songs and waving. These people have nothing, but everything. They ask for nothing and are content to live their primitive lives the way their ancestors have lived for hundreds of years. Thank God that the road had run out of money as it would have cut right through their lands and opened up the forest to intensive logging, which would have decimated the tribes.

Fortunately these are remote, inhospitable areas that are not conducive to the tourist industry. The pygmies made us welcome in their community, which was made up of individual dwellings built by bending branches and then covering them with leaves. The children were naked and the adults wore loin clothes made from animal skins. They cooked in the open and appeared to have no possessions other than the basic necessities they required to exist. They were not poor as they had everything that they needed. The patrol lasted two weeks and I was amazed at how many people lived in and off the forest.

One of the great things about these overseas postings was that we were never doing the same thing two days in a row. Our next assignment was in the capital Bangui, to guard key military installations at the airport, which also shared the runway with civilian traffic.

While we were there, we had an unexpected VIP to guard – the Pope. He was on a tour of African states and landed at Bangui airport. Being a sniper, I was positioned on top of a floodlight pylon and had a bird's-eye view of the proceedings. As he descended from the aircraft I couldn't help having a look at him through my telescopic sight and watched him in close-up as he made his now famous gesture of kissing the ground. Perhaps he hated flying.

He held a huge outdoor Mass in the local football stadium before he came back to the airport to continue his tour. After his departure, another sniper from one of the other groups said to me, 'Never tell any of my mates back home that I had the Pope in my sights.' He was a Protestant from Belfast and had left Northern Ireland to get away from the Troubles.

At the end of our third month we went back to Bouar to prepare for our return to Calvi. I had been told that I would be given the opportunity to go on a Caporals' course and started studying in preparation. The final weeks passed quickly and before we knew it we were on the plane heading back to France.

CHAPTER 8

Collective Power

Due to the increased intake over the past two years, there was an unusually large number of legionnaires from the REP due to go on a Caporals' course. Out of the forty places on the course, twenty had been allocated to the 'boys' from Calvi.

Our course was due to start on a Monday, with the last reporting time at Castelnaudary on the Sunday evening. Because of the sailing times from Corsica to the Continent at this time of the year, we were told that we would have to leave on the Wednesday night ferry from Bastia. This meant that we would arrive in Marseille early on Thursday morning and travel to Castelnaudary by train, arriving about 4.00 in the afternoon. We would be confined to camp for three days over the weekend before the course started which none of us wanted.

While on the ferry we got our heads together to discuss the problem and agreed that there was no way that we were going to let that happen. A plan of action was quickly agreed. We were being escorted by a Sergeant who had been tasked to deliver us directly to Castelnaudary, but we planned to ditch him in such a way that he would not be able do anything about it. If we worked together as a team, using our collective power, nothing could beat us.

The sea was calm and when we arrived at Marseille a bus was waiting for us on the quayside to take us to the railway station. We all boarded the train as planned and settled back to enjoy the run along the coast. Before reaching Narbonne, the last stop before the train headed inland on its run up to Toulouse, we made sure that the Sergeant was well established in the buffet car. He had no reason to suspect that we were up to anything and was enjoying a drink with a crowd of us around him for company.

When the train stopped, Operation 'Ditch the Sergeant' was put into action. Timing was everything. Half a dozen of our group got out at the front of the train and walked slowly back down the platform towards the buffet car. In France, as previously pointed out, a three-minute stop means exactly that – not a second more, not a second less. Thirty seconds before the train was due to pull out of the station, our six volunteers walked past the buffet car window and waved at those inside.

We made sure that the Sergeant saw them, he shot off his bar stool, ran for the nearest door and was out on the platform about five seconds before the train doors closed behind him. Once closed there was no way that they could be reopened. The door of the last carriage meanwhile was being held open by one of our group and the last of the six swung up into the train as it started to roll.

The next thing the sergeant was aware of was the train pulling out of the station with not a Legionnaire in sight on the platform. When he looked up there were twenty legionnaires waving at him from the departing train, leaving him standing on the platform without his kepi, his bags and most important of all, his detachment of legionnaires. I must admit that I felt sorry for him. He was the innocent victim of a well-organized plot.

The worst that could happen to us was that we would all be thrown off the course and sent back to Calvi. For the sergeant, I wasn't so sure. We were all a bit nervous as the train pulled in to Castelnaudary. We half expected the Military Police to board the train to escort us all to the camp, but we needn't have worried, there was no sign of them. I suppose up to that point we hadn't done anything wrong.

We all stayed on the train to Toulouse where we went our separate ways for some unofficial leave. Some got on the TGV for Paris, others like myself decided to stay on in what was France's second largest city. I had never been there before and there was lots to do. Being so close to Castelnaudary, legionnaires in uniform were not unusual.

We spent our time relaxing, bought some extra equipment to use on the course, went to the cinema and had a couple of good meals. On the Sunday morning, as agreed, we all headed for Castelnaudary, arriving at the station a little after 11.00. A reception committee was waiting for us as we stepped off the train. A sergeant chef, a sergeant and four MPs from the Training Regiment were standing on the platform. They wanted to take us to the camp in dribs and drabs as the lads arrived, but we had agreed that we would all regroup at the station and go to the camp together. Our strength was in our solidarity and we refused to go. There were only four still to arrive and their train was due in about five minutes, so we stayed. The REP has a mean reputation and the young MPs were afraid to take us on. Six against sixteen was no contest.

The final four arrived on time and we got onto the lorries for the short drive to the camp. When the lorries stopped at the main gates we all jumped down and lined up in two rows to march into the camp. Again the MPs were taken by surprise and could do nothing about it. The gates opened and we marched onto the parade square singing the REP regimental song. The sentries and the MPs were obliged by tradition to stand to attention and salute as we marched past.

Unbeknown to us, our second in command from the REP, Lieutenant Colonel Halbert, had flown by helicopter from Calvi and was waiting to interview us one at a time. He must have been watching from a window as we marched proudly into the camp. We were kept standing on the parade square for four hours before the interviews began, during which time we were not allowed to talk while we waited our turn, or question those who had been interviewed and returned to the ranks.

We gradually became aware that we were being watched from the windows of the barracks by those undergoing their basic training. Everyone was confined to quarters while all of this was going on. Quite what they thought of us we will never know, but I am sure that they must have been impressed.

I was second last to go in for questioning and by now it was just after six in the evening. We hadn't eaten or been given any water, although fortunately for us it was a sunny but cool day. I am sure that we would have been left standing there even if it had been raining or even snowing.

After being marched in, the Colonel simply asked me to explain what we had done and why we had done it. He did not raise his voice or show any sign of displeasure at what had happened. In fact I got the impression that he was quite pleased that we had stuck together and had enhanced the reputation of the Regiment as being something special, to be held in awe by those not part of it. When I had finished my explanation he said that we would be staying to do the course and that any disciplinary action would be taken by the Regiment on our return. He also made it clear that he expected us all to come out at the top of the course and that nothing else would be good enough.

It was decided by the Colonel in Chief of the Training Regiment that everyone from the REP would be kept together for the course in one section. He felt that it would not be fair to those from the other regiments to be dominated by the 'REPmen'. Basically, he thought they could break us that way. Half of us were Brits or English speaking, and that was another bond within our group.

First thing on the Monday morning we were assembled before our own Colonel in private. He told us that he could not condone what we had done, but he was pleased that we had stuck together. We were now expected to return his trust with positive results on the course, both as a group and as individuals, in the name of the Regiment. At the end of the course any punishment would reflect our achievements.

The only people to suffer immediate sanctions were the Sergeant who had been in charge of us and the Legionnaire who had been carrying our paperwork and had left it on the train. Fortunately it had been recovered but they were both sent back to Calvi. The Sergeant was demoted for six months but the Legionnaire was back at Castelnaudary on the next course.

Fortunately we had good NCO instructors. Two of them were ex-REP and wanted to return, while the others had ambitions to be transferred there. It was good to know that they were on our side and would be working with us rather than against. It was going to be an interesting four months. Our fitness levels were far superior to those of the other section and probably that of our instructors. We were going to be doing all our training at the farm where I had done my basic training and I therefore had another advantage of knowing the terrain. We were soon well into the programme of instruction and there was a healthy competitive atmosphere right from the start. It was also clear from the beginning that there were at least half a dozen natural leaders in our section who would challenge for first place. Instruction was comprehensive and intensive, and our group thrived on it. Every challenge was met head on as a united unit while individual skills came to the fore.

Time passed quickly and we were soon starting the final month of tests. The written and practical tests went well, but the most important test of all was the 30k forced march against the clock. Normally it would be every man for himself and the two sections combined for this final push. Right from the beginning of the course our section had worked together as a team, helping the weakest of us to perform well. On top of that we were 'The men from the REP', and we all knew that the Regiment expected us to stick together. There were those amongst us who were more than capable of setting a record time for the march but we all remembered the last words of the Colonel before he left. This was about regimental supremacy. The fittest helped the weakest who by any standards were fitter than many top athletes. We worked as a group with each of us taking it in turn to set the pace.

By the halfway stage most of the other section had been left behind and there were some very good lads amongst them. They were not given the cold shoulder by the rest of us and were encouraged to join in on the teamwork.

It is traditional for the Colonel in Chief of the 4eme RE and his senior officers, to come to the finish of the march to congratulate the winner. We all knew who was going to come top overall in the course and he had nothing left to prove. We therefore stopped before the final bend, out of sight of those waiting at the finish, and formed up into two columns. Our colleague who was going to come first then led us in. We were perfectly aligned, jogging in step and chanting our own version of 'Two old ladies lying in bed, one rolled over and the other one said', in English.

The look on the faces of the officers was worth all the effort. At first they didn't know how to react – this had never happened before – but as we crossed the line they burst into applause. It was great to finish the course like this and we were elated that it was all over. We all gathered at the finish line to encourage the rest of the course as they straggled home in dribs and drabs. The last home was almost three quarters of an hour behind our group. In a way it was a shame because none of the participants had done badly, it was just that once more we had demonstrated that we, the 'REPmen', had earned the reputation of being part of an elite regiment.

We couldn't wait to get back to Calvi to learn our fate. We occupied the top fifteeen places and the lowest finished twenty-second. I finished ninth which was a good result considering that I was rapidly approaching forty.

When we got back to Calvi we formed up before our Colonel in Chief, Colonel Germanos. He congratulated us on our results but could not resist adding that it was only what he had expected and that he would have accepted nothing less. Colonel Germanos was the perfect example of a Legion officer, and was loved and respected by us all. He would go on to become a five-star general and overall commander of all of the French armed forces.

As for our indiscretion on the way to the course, he told us that we would return to our duties as acting Caporals, but without the stripes or increase in pay. He and he alone would decide if and when we got promoted.

There had been an attempted coup in the Republic of Central Africa and the country was far from stable. The Regiment was on G1 alert and it was decided by Paris that we should reinforce the French troops based there. We would have to ensure the safety, and if necessary, the evacuation of all foreigners working in the country.

Two days after arriving back in Calvi we were on our way to Africa again. When we arrived at the airport in Bangui there were local troops everywhere and the atmosphere was electric. Half of them seemed to be high on drugs or alcohol and were trigger happy. It is at times like this that the REP's reputation as being a hard, uncompromising fighting unit can help to save lives. None of the locals were prepared to take us on and an element of normality was quickly restored round the airport. We installed a half-mile no-go area round the facility, ensuring that anyone entering the area was disarmed. Patrols were sent out to key installations and to the foreign workers' residences to protect them from the drunken armed gangs that were roaming the streets.

There were a couple of short exchanges of fire without injury to our guys and that was enough to quell any resistance. The coup collapsed quickly after that and the country got back to normal. It was decided that we should stay on in the country until they were sure that the uprising was well and truly over.

We went back to our old base in Bouar and found everything more or less as we had left it just over six months earlier. Because we were surplus to requirements we had little or nothing to do, so it was decided that we would use the time to do some jungle training. We spent the next three weeks deep in the tropical forest learning how to live off the land with no logistical support. It was fantastic. We were introduced to some pretty awesome animals and insects, but the most impressive were the snakes. Big spiders I can deal with, but huge snakes are something else

It was while we were there that word came through that I had officially been promoted. The last twelve months had flown past so quickly that I did not realize I had not been on leave for a year. I wasn't complaining but was looking forward to our return to Calvi for a bit of a break.

A couple of weeks later we were heading back to Calvi.

CHAPTER 9

Commando Training

This is where we return to the action at the end of Chapter 1. Eventually my hood was removed and the interrogation began in earnest. The questions were as you would have expected in the real thing. 'Where are you from? What is your unit? What is their strength? What is you mission?' I replied with the normal name, rank and number, but was truly shocked when the interrogation turned violent. It took me totally by surprise even though I should have known better. If all the other training was realistic, why shouldn't this be? I was given an open-handed slap with such force that it knocked me backwards, causing me to fall over the back of the bench onto the floor. It was hard enough to draw blood and had the effect of making me take this part of the exercise very seriously.

After ten minutes of what can only be described as very robust questioning by my interrogators, they suddenly left. They turned off the lights as they did so, but during the last few minutes I had started to take in my surroundings. Apart from anything else it helped to focus the mind on something other than the interrogation. They obviously expected me to try and escape so there had to be a way out of the room.

I was being held in a large room with a huge stone fireplace. It was obviously the older part of the fort because of the stone walls and high ceiling. The only window was about 15 feet above the floor level and barred. I could see the sky was beginning to lighten. I had lost track of time but it was obviously early morning and it was going to be a long day.

I slipped my hands under my feet to bring them out in front before using a sharp corner stone in the fireplace to cut through the plastic tag round my wrists. I tried the door on the off chance – sometimes the obvious is overlooked, but not in this case. That only left the chimney.

It was a huge affair that could have been used to roast a pig on a spit over the fire. When I looked inside I could see a small glimmer of light but it was a long way up. The chimney was certainly wide enough but it would be quite a climb. Even if I could have got out that way there was a 150-foot drop from the roof into the moat. Oh well, give it a go – that was why I was there!

It took me all of fifteen minutes, with much sweat and skinned knees, to get to the top. The chimney was capped and although I could see out it was not my escape route. As I struggled back down I became aware that in fact it served two separate fireplaces. I had not noticed it on the way up but the second chimney took me down to a room below the one I had been held in.

The descent was a lot easier physically but if I lost my grip it was a long way to fall. My back and feet were braced against either side of the chimney and I was greatly relieved when I stepped into the fireplace. The room was in total darkness and there were no windows, so I guessed that I was below ground level. I worked my way round the walls until I came to a large oak door. To my relief it wasn't locked. No one intercepted me, but I knew that they must be watching and I had to progress to part two of the exercise – getting out of the fort.

It was freezing cold and the sky was crystal clear. There were still a couple of hours before the sun would show its head above the mountains. If I was to get clear I would have to do it quickly, and I had to get warmer clothing, so instead of making an immediate attempt to escape, I made my way back to my room. Everyone else was obviously getting the same treatment and the room was empty. I quickly changed into my thermal boots and cold-weather gear, then filled my small backpack with what I thought I might need to survive the first couple of days. Weight would also be a factor while negotiating the obstacles on my way over the wall.

The obstacle courses we had been practising on was now my way out of the fort. There had been a heavy snowfall the previous evening, it was now well below freezing and most of the surfaces were brick hard and very slippery. Everything has a plus side and the hard ground made it easier to cover my tracks. I did not know how much time they would allow for me to get clear before the chase would start. My plan was to find somewhere close at hand to lie up for the first day. A lot of people make the mistake of trying to run ahead of the pack instead of going to ground. It would also give me the chance to observe what kind of opposition I could expect. I knew that there would be search parties out looking for us and that the Gendarmerie would also be taking part in the exercise in the same way they would be if it was the real thing. The Gendarmerie, like all of the French emergency services, are part of the military. There was therefore automatic inter-arm cooperation for this kind of exercise. Even the local population were aware of what was going on, so I could not rely on any help there.

Part of our brief was that if we managed to escape we should make our way to a particular location where we would join up with other escapees for the third part of the exercise. If we had not made it to the rendezvous point by the end of the third day, we should give ourselves up to the Police, having successfully stayed undetected for the required period.

It took me about three quarters of an hour to make my way over the inner wall and moat, which was frozen, then down a cable slide over the outer wall and into the woods on the north side of the fort. I was now in the outer grounds but still had to negotiate the tripwire alert system and get past the outer fence. If I tripped the system it would set off flares and I wouldn't get far after that. We had been training to break into the fort through this area just a couple of days earlier. In or out, it was the same.

I cleared the area and headed deeper into the woods, making sure that I left some tracks, before circling back towards the town hopefully without leaving any. It would be easier to find somewhere to hide up in some of the old outbuildings, many of which should be empty at this time of year. It would also be a lot warmer than trying to lie up outdoors.

Dogs are your worst enemy when trying to move about populated areas at odd hours, but like their owners, they seemed to be indoors out of the cold. I soon found an old barn-cum-outhouse with a loft storage area. The house seemed uninhabited and it did not appear as if anyone had been here for some time. Perfect. The doors were held closed by a chain and padlock but it was slack enough for me to push my pack through before squeezing in after it. It was like stepping into a time warp. The only light filtering into the ground floor came from the gap in the doors but I could see that it was full of old farm equipment and hand tools that would have been worth a fortune to a collector. They must have been lying here untouched for over thirty years.

There was hardly room to move as I made my way to the stairs that led to the loft space. It was not much better but a little light was coming in via a half-open shutter on the only window. When I eventually managed to get close enough to the window to look out I could see that it gave me a clear view of the comings and goings at the fort. I couldn't have found a better place.

Although this was an exercise, the ground rules laid down were pretty strict. You could not use public transport or thumb a lift as you were supposedly in enemy uniform and in time of war that would not have been possible. You were not allowed to break any laws. If I had forced the door to gain entry to my hide, or stolen any clothes or food, I would have to face any civil action that might be taken if I was caught.

It would have been easier just to stay put for the three days but you gained marks for your efforts to reach the rendezvous point. I would rest up for the remainder of the day and move out after dark. It was still exceptionally cold but at least I was out of the snow and wind.

There was a stone fireplace downstairs which I used to make some hot soup from my ration pack and the heating tablets from my survival kit. You just placed them on a suitable surface, lit them and used them like a stove. They gave out no smoke to give you away and I warmed my hands up as I prepared the soup.

Back upstairs I cleared a space by the window before enjoying the hot drink. I took my boots off before getting into my lightweight, Gore-tex bivi bag and was soon sound asleep. Being able to sleep when you can is a skill that soldiers develop, especially when on guard duty. Sleep, guard, sleep, guard. If you don't you quickly become overtired and can't operate effectively.

It was mid-afternoon when I woke up. Before getting out of my sleeping bag I had a bar of chocolate and made my plans for the next part of the exercise. I didn't have a map but it was not difficult to work out which direction I wanted to go in: downhill. As darkness fell I packed everything away and made sure that I had left no sign of my passing. It was time to go.

It had not snowed any more but it was still extremely cold. I slipped out of my hiding place and made my way southwards out of town. It was important to keep away from the roads as there would be mobile patrols and fixed observation points set up at key points along the route. I made good progress for the first couple of hours but was aware that I was entering the danger zone. I was getting into that period when you begin to relax and as a result take risks that would end in failure. It was easy to walk straight into a trap.

Over the past ten hours I had descended from the highest part of the mountains to a high plateau. I had a deep gorge to cross and there were few places to do it safely without being seen. From the edge of the forest I watched the area around a road bridge for over half an hour, looking for signs of an observation post. I couldn't see anything but that meant nothing, so I took extra care as I worked my way towards the bridge.

I kept well inside the tree line and although I couldn't see them I suddenly heard the unmistakable sound of a camping gas stove hissing just a few yards from me. I froze immediately before retracing my steps until I was well away from the observation post before setting out to find another way across the gorge.

The presence of this OP confirmed my suspicions that as we were on an escape and evasion exercise, another regiment must have been set the task of catching us. That added an extra edge to what was going on. I couldn't let the REP down by getting caught, especially if it was a Regular Army unit involved.

Half an hour after passing the observation post I spotted a foot patrol crossing a field. I kept down behind a wall, lying flat in the tall grass for almost ten minutes to be sure that they had moved on. I counted the number in the group to be sure that they had not split up. This was good practice as the following members of the group would spot you as you moved out thinking it was safe.

I had to cross the gorge and I had to do it soon. My chance came when I came on what seemed like a small quarry or mine. There was a single cable stretching across the gorge which was obviously used like a crane to transport material from one side to the other. It took me a few minutes to establish that the site was not in use before I set out to cross the gorge using the cable. There was a 30-foot drop to the floor of the ravine and the river which passed through the centre. It was no different to the obstacles we had been training on at Fort Louis.

Security is important, especially on real operations. You are no good to your mission if you fall off an obstacle while trying to cross it. I took my belt off and lengthened it to the maximum. It was easy to get onto the cable and I hooked my belt round myself and the cable for security before setting out to cross. It took me only a couple of minutes to get to the other side and nobody jumped out to capture me.

Despite the cold I was sweating as a result of my exertions. This in itself was a problem, as hypothermia could set in due to my damp clothes. I would have to find a place to hide up and get dried out. I walked for ten minutes away from my normal line of march and found a small copse in front of a rock face which would prevent anyone coming upon me from behind. The other good news was that the area was crawling with rabbits. I made a couple of snares and withdrew from the area I had set them in to prepare my hide. There was a deep cleft at the base of the rock face, not quite a cave but enough to give me shelter.

I gathered some dry wood and soon had a smokeless fire going with the aid of a heating tablet from my survival pack. I changed into some dry underwear and got into my bivi bag to warm up. An hour later I got up, got dressed and went to check the snares. I was delighted to see that I had caught my lunch. I found a small stream close by and after breaking the ice, skinned and cleaned the rabbit in readiness for cooking. If anyone passed too close to my hiding place they would have smelt the aroma of cooking rabbit, but that was a chance I was prepared to take.

I checked the rabbit at regular intervals until it was properly cooked – the last thing I wanted was food poisoning. The smell was delicious and I realized I was ravenous. After the meal I cleaned up all traces of my cooking and would do an other sweep before I left. It was always important to make sure that you left no trace of your passage. On a previous training exercise our instructors had scoured our camp after we had left, then presented us with all the information they had gleamed from our rubbish and odd things that had been thrown away. This ranged from the name of our Regiment which was printed for all to see on the side of a disposable lighter, to what direction we had taken from the trail of cigarette ends from that final smoke as we left camp.

I was awakened in the mid-afternoon by voices. It took me a moment or two to realize where I was as the voices came closer. I was confident that they would not find my hide as I had taken time to camouflage it properly before I settled down for a kip. I couldn't see anyone but they were very close. It is amazing how loud your breathing sounds to yourself when you are trying to be quiet. The group were now so close to me that I could make out what they were saying. They were not behaving in a manner that made me think that they were aware of my presence. There were some bramble bushes just in front of my hiding place and this gave me some additional natural cover. From the number of footsteps I could tell that this was a military group and not just some civilians passing by.

As the voices and footsteps receded I slowly let out my breath. I hadn't realized that I had been holding it. My earlier attention to detail had paid off. I stayed in place until dark and had a hot drink before heading off towards the rendezvous point. The going was easier now and I made good time as I moved downhill.

We had been briefed on the final phase of the exercise at the start of the week and I knew that the aim was to attack a hydroelectric dam. This also made it easier to find as all I had to do was follow the valley until I came to a lake. We were to be given dummy explosive charges to place on the wall of the dam before making a tactical retreat. I had until midnight to make it to the dam and join up with anyone else who had successfully made their escape.

The moon was up and the sky was crystal clear when I moved into the area. It was very cold and I had tied a handkerchief over my mouth to hide the giveaway trace of steam rising from my breath. The timing of the mission was planned to catch any guards at the lowest point of their alertness, which was always about five in the morning. I knew only too well what it was like to do guard duty at that time of the morning – you were cold, half asleep and bored witless.

Just after two thirty I heard then saw a couple of figures moving slowly down the hillside about 20 yards to my left, but waited until they drew level with me before making them aware of my presence. Over the next couple of hours our numbers grew as we waited to be contacted by our instructors.

When a jeep drove into the clearing, I could make out our instructors and watched as they got a small fire going. They put what looked like a large coffee pot onto the glowing embers. It was time to join them. They also had a large urn full of hot soup waiting for us and checked off our names as they handed us a mug. Boy, was it good. My rabbit meal seemed like ages ago and the soup went down well.

After a short briefing they handed out the dummy explosives and a set of plans showing the layout of the hydroelectric system. It was we who had to plan the attack and work out where the explosives should be placed to cause the maximum damage. The plan was to destroy the generating capacity rather than rupture the dam. There were several towns further down the valley and if this had been for real it would not be the aim of the mission to cause massive loss of life to the civilian population.

An hour later we attacked the dam, neutralizing the guards before abseiling down the face of the dam to gain access to the huge outflow pipes directly below the generators. Another reason for the timing of the attack was that at this early hour there was not the demand for electricity and the turbines were not working. Another couple of hours and the station would see the turbines working flat out and it would have not have been possible to go inside the pipes to place the charges.

The charges were what we called flash-bangs as when we detonated them they let off a very loud bang and a bright flash to simulate an explosion but did not cause any real damage. With the mission accomplished we made a tactical withdrawal before regrouping back at the clearing. Our instructors seemed to be pleased enough with our efforts as we embarked on the lorries for the journey back up the mountain to Mont Louis.

After a short debriefing and a thorough medical, we enjoyed a hearty breakfast before crawling into our beds for a good sleep. The course was over and there was nothing left to do but get our equipment together for the return trip to Calvi. We travelled back down to the coast by lorry to the air base at Perpignan, where three C160 Transalls were waiting to fly us back to our base. As members of a parachute regiment it was only right that we would be jumping back into our camp as the climax to the course.

A little over three quarters of an hour after taking off, we were on the final approach to the drop zone. The aircraft had formed up in close formation one behind the other in combat jump formation. It was also the practice to make this as close to real combat as possible and we would be jumping at 300 metres.

It was a small drop zone with a normal stick being ten parachutists per door per pass, i.e. twenty in the air at a time. The jump masters were Regular Army and had not been briefed about what was about to happen. When the red light came on they called for the ten per stick to stand up and hook on. To their astonishment everyone stood up and hooked on.

With the aircraft rapidly approaching the drop zone, the jump masters were frantically trying to get the rest of us to sit down. Exactly the same thing was happening on the other two aircraft and when the green light came on, the jump started. It was like a rugby scrum and with everyone pushing from behind, the aircraft emptied in under thirty seconds. With the other aircraft close behind, there were 120 parachutists in the air at the same time. The jump masters had to stand back and let it happen or they would have been out of the doors as well. This was six times the normal number of parachutists in the air at any one time, but it was exactly what would have happened in time of war. When the air is so crowded you take extra care and pay more attention to what is happening around you. As a result everyone landed safely. When a complete company is jumping back into Calvi, everyone comes out to watch and it also tends to cause a traffic jam on the main road into Calvi as the cars stop to view the spectacle. This was what it meant to be part of the Legion's most elite regiment – everyone was on a high.

Once everything had been cleaned and put back into store we had to get changed into our dress uniforms for the presentation ceremony at which our Colonel in Chief presented the 'Commando Entraînement' badges to those of us who had successfully completed the course. I felt quite chuffed at having made it. Each combat company has its own speciality and courses. Everyone wore their specialist badges with pride, inter-company rivalry was fierce and it was rare for anyone to want to move between combat companies.

Within a month of being back in Calvi I was posted to the Bureau Operations and Instruction unit, known as the BOI. This meant leaving the 1st Company for the Regiment's Command Company, the CCS. The BOI was a small specialized unit responsible for all operational planning, specialist instruction, situation analysis, mapping and photography. My new responsibilities included keeping up to date all maps and information on areas in the world where we might become involved. I had to build up a library of satellite photographs which I obtained from a variety of sources, including the National Geographical Institute, the French equivalent of the Ordnance Survey in the UK. I also had access to various military sources worldwide. All this was quite a responsibility as it was important that we had the latest information to hand instantly.

My old artistic skills were brought into use, allowing me to prepare graphic presentations for the Regiment to a standard they were not used to.

This was of particular use to the Colonel in Chief when he was making presentations to visiting VIPs. It also meant that I was present at most of these presentations and performed the additional duty of interpreter when we had foreign visitors. To help me perform this new duty, I was sent to qualify as an official army interpreter. This qualification (Certificat Technique Premier Degré) meant that my security clearance was upgraded, and I got another pay rise. It also made my work more interesting as I was now privy to everything that was happening in the Regiment. The one drawback was that I was very, very busy and every time I was proposed for a sergeants' course, something would come up a couple of days before I was due to go. I complained to my department boss who expressed his sympathy, but nothing changed.

After three years' service you go through a process called rectification in which your personal details, such as your real name, age and nationality, are reinstated. I had gone through this as part of my new security status, but it meant that I was back to my real age and was thus barred from the sergeants' course, which you had to start before the age of forty. There was not a thing I could do about it, but it was a bit of a downer all the same.

On 18 June 1944, General de Gaulle of France had made his famous speech from London about France being occupied but not defeated. This speech is now celebrated by the French every year and the occasion is used in much the same way as the Queen's Birthday is in the UK to distribute honours and awards. As part of this tradition every year all regiments assemble and the speech is read out to them by the Colonel in Chief. On 18 June 1988, immediately after this had been done, I was called out before the assembled Regiment and promoted to the rank of Caporal Chef by special order, with immediate effect. I didn't know that it was going to happen and was deeply honoured — it went a long way towards compensating me for being blocked from the sergeants' course. Normally this rank was not achieved until you had at least ten years' service and I had less than five. It also gave me another pay rise so I wasn't about to complain.

The rank of Caporal Chef is a NCO rank which entitles you to quite a few privileges, such as living out of camp, buying a car, opening a bank account or getting married. It also allowed me to take charge of a combat group and to perform tasks normally associated with higher ranks.

At the beginning of July that year, the Regiment went back to Tchad for a normal four-month deployment. I was attached to the 3rd Company as a Chef-de-Group in one of the combat sections. We were to be stationed at Abéché which was close to the frontier with Sudan. As already described, I like the desert and had been stationed at Abéché on my first visit to Tchad in

1984. I was surprised when some of the locals with whom we had worked before remembered me by name.

There were no particular problems in the area this time and it gave us the chance to train extensively in the art of desert warfare. We took over from a Regular Army unit and as usual we found that nothing had been done to the camp to improve the living conditions. They had been living in what can only be described as squalor rather than make the effort to improve things for themselves. Wherever the Legion goes they try to improve on and make the most of what they have. Within days of our arrival mud bricks were baking in the sun and the first real accommodation blocks had been constructed by the end of the second week. We begged and borrowed anything that could be used or adapted to improve our lot. We found the generator that we had acquired for our old camp in 1984 – it was still there where we had left it. Because it was petrol driven it was of no use to the locals and was in perfect condition as nothing rusts in the desert. We soon had it going and persuaded the Air Force to donate another one in exchange for the right to visit us, and share our recreational facilities together with some of our well-known hospitality whenever they wanted. Fuel for the generators was at a premium but we only required power for a couple of hours in the evening to run some lighting and the video system we had installed in the mess.

By the end of the month we had completely rebuilt the whole camp with separate messes for the officers, NCOs and a first-class kitchen, mess and recreational facilities for the legionnaires. New entrance gates were erected and a parade-cum-sports area cleared in the centre of the camp. The morale of the company was lifted and on the whole, life was very acceptable.

The principal reason for our presence in Tchad was to maintain the security of the frontier and guard the military facilities at the air base which had two Mirage fighter aircraft and a C160 Transall on permanent station. The fighters flew daily missions along the Libyan frontier and had the habit of buzzing the base at a very low altitude at the end of each mission. Despite warnings by the base commander, this somewhat dangerous practice continued until he asked for our help. It was time that the cocky pilots were put in their places.

The base was protected from ground attack by 5-metre-high earth banks and after landing the aircraft had to taxi through them to gain access to the parking area and hangars. The fighters had to stop briefly before passing through the gap to enable the ground crews to make safe the air-to-ground missiles. While the aircraft were stationary a couple of our lads ran out unseen by the pilots and attached to the aircraft about 30 metres of cable of the type which was normally used on the aerial farm. After they taxied in, the pilots were met on the tarmac by a supposedly irate officer from the signals unit who proceeded to dress them down, pointing out the trail of wire snagged under the aircraft. The pilots protested their innocence and neither of them twigged that they had been set up until much later. The message got across and it put an end to the practice of low flying. It was all taken good humouredly but could have ended in tears if they had got caught up in the aerial farm for real.

We had the chance to discover the real joys of the desert on a two-week patrol deep into the Sahara. As we were forbidden to sleep on the vehicles in case of air attack, we laid out our sleeping bags in the sand in a circle round the vehicles and slept under the stars, which was wonderful.

One night we stopped as usual just before dark and set up our camp under some palm trees. After the evening meal I posted the guard and issued them with night-vision goggles, with which you could pick out the faintest stars far away in space. It was a breathtaking sight. I suppose that the same thing must be experienced in the middle of the ocean. The glasses could also pick out the faintest light sources far out in the desert. It always came as a surprise just how many people were camped out there. You thought that you were on your own in the middle of nowhere, but it was far from the case. Nomadic caravans still criss-cross the desert as they have done for centuries.

One afternoon we had watched a nomadic caravan pass us while we were having a break. It was an entire village on the move, complete with goats and dozens of camels which just seemed to amble along at their own pace. They wouldn't stop until they reached the next oasis where the animals could graze. The men walked in front of their camels leading the whole village along at a calm walking pace. The women and children were on the backs of camels protected from the sun by material stretched over a frame. The only sounds came from the camels who kind of snorted as they were led along, their huge feet spreading out over the sand to take the weight. They walked with an economy of movement under the blazing sun. It was over 40°C in the shade, but even we were getting used to it. It took almost three hours for the camel train to pass through our location.

By contrast the night temperature dropped very quickly as the sand give up its heat and after the evening meal everyone wasted no time in getting into the warmth of their sleeping bags. Whereas some read for a while by torchlight, I was more than content to lay back and stare at the stars. It was mesmerizing, to say the least – almost hypnotic – and you were made to feel very small in the overall scale of things. You soon fell asleep under nature's fairylights.

At about 2.00 one morning I was jolted out of my sleep by someone swearing loudly and by torches being switched on all over the place. The sand was moving with hundreds of large black scorpions. They had been drawn to our campsite in search of heat and were trying to get into the sleeping bags beside the legionnaires. To hell with regulations – everyone was given the order to get into the vehicles. No one had been bitten and the sleeping bags were all turned inside out to evict any unwelcome guests.

Because of the intensity of the sun, everyone had to keep their sleeves rolled down and their skin covered as much as possible. The temptation was to do the opposite to try and keep cool, but it was amazing how effective the nomadic headwear was when worn correctly. Despite all these precautions I still got sunburn on the tip of my nose and on the outside of my ears. It was very painful and I had to keep the affected areas well covered in cream.

I love Africa despite the extremes of climate and the landscapes – from the mountains of Tibesti and the sands of the Sahara, to the tropical forests. Huge red ants, spiders, scorpions, snakes and elephants – it didn't matter what they were, they were fabulous. There were occasions we would rather have forgotten, like the huge, suffocating, hot sandstorms that got into every orifice you could imagine; or the swarms of flies and mosquitoes that would cover you from head to toe given half a chance. But these were a small price to pay for the privilege of visiting this wonderful continent.

Only too quickly it was time to head back to Calvi.

CHAPTER 10

New Responsibilities

On our return to Calvi we were given the usual month's leave, the difference this time being that my new rank let me take mine anywhere in the world that I wanted. I went back to Scotland for a couple of weeks but was soon fed up and headed back to the south of France and spent the time exploring the area round Nice. I hired a car and visited all the small coastal towns from Nice to the Italian border. You can't visit this area without spending some time in Monaco. Just walking round the port, looking at how the other half live is a real eye-opener. The mega yachts were something else and I personally don't mind how much they cost. They provide employment for lots of people from boatbuilders and crews, to florists and those who supply their basic provisions at every port of call. Who cares what the owners do? As long as they spend their money everyone is happy.

When I returned to Calvi after my leave I expected to return to my old duties at the BOI but instead I was asked to take over the 'Cellule Audiovisuelle', or 'Photographic Unit'. The Sergeant in charge was being posted to Aubagne to work as the photographer for the Legion magazine, *Le Kepi Blanc*. This was a great opportunity for me and a particularly interesting career move. It meant that I would be involved in every exercise and operation which the Regiment would get involved in. The intention was that I would expand the scope of the unit to include my previous duties and help to introduce some of the new military photographic technology that was becoming available. It would be an enormous workload but I was looking forward to the challenge.

The 'Cellule' consisted of a fifty-seater theatre where presentations and briefings took place. It was equipped with two giant TV monitors and an overhead projection system. There was a dark room for black and white development, a photo studio, file room and front office.

I also had responsibility for the combat simulator unit called the 'Cine-Tir' – an indoor shooting range that had a film projection system. Combat situations were projected onto a large screen which was in fact two rolls of heavy duty paper about 2 inches apart. As the film rolled, legionnaires fired at moving targets in a variety of combat situations, from urban to open terrain, using their normal assault rifles while using ammunition with a plastic tip. When they fired, the projectile penetrated the two rolls of paper. The sound of the shot stopped the film and a light came on at the back of the system which let you see the exact point of impact. The projectile impacted harmlessly against a concrete wall and after a short delay the paper rolls moved 5cm in opposite directions before the film recommenced. It could also be used with anti-tank weapons which were fitted with a converter that fired the same ammunition as a rifle as you obviously couldn't fire the real thing on an outdoor range. The facility was well used by the Regiment and the local Gendarmerie used it for side-arm training. Some of the films were very good and would simulate a hostage situation in which you could fire at the hostage taker under circumstances you wouldn't dare risk in real-life situations. Every year the Regiment had a procurement budget which had to be spent by a particular date. If it was not used by then, the allocation for the following year would be reduced by the surplus, but as can be imagined, things were normally found to spend it on. Up until then the 'Cellule Audiovisuelle' had not been used to support operations and had no specialized military photographic equipment. I wanted to introduce equipment that was used to gather intelligence that could be developed in situ on actual operations, or sent back to base electronically in real time by satellite. Digital photography was a new technology at this time and the system I was looking at did not come cheap. The Regiment had been overseas for much of the year and had not spent its budget allocation. If you don't ask you don't get, so I put in a requisition order for almost £100,000 worth of equipment in the hope that I might get at least part of it. I was therefore astonished when I got everything on my list, which in itself led to another problem – I had no idea how to use it. I had read all about the advantages of the technology and about the great things it could do, but that's not quite the same thing.

I managed to get on a surveillance equipment course being run by a specialist arm of the Gendarmerie in Paris, the GIGN (Groupe d'Intervention Gendarmerie National) and spent a month with them. Apart from learning how to use the equipment, they took me along as an observer on some of their operations. The Legion and the Gendarmerie have always enjoyed an excellent relationship and I had worked with some of these guys before when they came to Calvi on exercise.

It was a month well spent and seemed to fly past. Back in Calvi I wasted no time in getting my new toys into operation. My first task was to introduce the equipment to and train selected members of the CRAP, which was an unfortunate abbreviation for Le Commando de Renseignement et Action dans la Profondeur (Deep Reconnaissance Commando Group). This was the title of the small special operations unit which, although only thirty strong, had a reputation for being one of the best special forces units in the world.

The unit was trained to operate well behind enemy lines, gathering information, destroying key installations or on diplomatic protection and hostage release. Methods of infiltration varied from high-altitude parachute drops day or night, to amphibious landings and helicopter assaults. The unit had specialist commando and support skills, and individual members were experts in signals, a variety of weapons, explosives, mapping and first aid. The unit was made up of men from a diversity of nationalities and cultural backgrounds, which meant that there were not many languages that were not spoken, or at least understood by someone in the group.

They were a great team to work with and never made me feel inferior. Because the equipment was so new and still evolving, it was decided that it was easier to train me to become part of the team than the other way round. This would mean me having to qualify in freefall parachuting and passing the same physical tests, including being able to cover 30 kilometres in full combat gear in under three hours while carrying a 15-kilo pack and weapon. The course in Calvi started at sea level, went over a pass at 300 metres, then back downhill, ending in the camp. The object of the test was not to do it in a couple of hours and be out on your feet at the end, it was to finish as quickly as you could within the time and still be capable of completing a mission.

Again this was an example of where my age was an advantage rather than an obstacle. My endurance levels were very good and I found it easier than many of my super-fit colleagues. The parachute training took place on the mainland at the French national parachute training centre at Pau. It was one of the best courses I have ever done and apart from learning the skills, it was fun. Back behind my desk in the 'Cellule Audiovisuelle', I settled down to the normal life of the Regiment.

During this period we had a visit from the head of the French Army during our annual inspection. Part of this included a presentation by our Colonel in Chief to explain the strengths and weaknesses of the Regiment. The CIC explained that a considerable number of ex-British soldiers had joined the Regiment immediately after the Falklands War and that these men posed a particular challenge. If there was trouble on the base it seemed that the Brits were always behind it. The problem was that they became bored quickly, but if you worked them into the ground they were the best soldiers he had – no matter how hard he worked them, they always came back for more.

My closest friend had just completed his sergeants' course and was now attached to the 2nd Company, which specialized in mountain warfare. We both had flats in the same block and bought motorbikes which we felt was the best way to see the island. I bought a second-hand 250cc Honda trials bike, but my friend bought a brand-new 1,100cc Yamaha flying machine which became his pride and joy. The bikes were kept in a private car park at the back of our blocks and were not visible to casual passers-by.

One morning when we came down the Yamaha was missing. We reported the theft to the Police and two days later it was found lying on the beach. It had been driven along the railway line that ran just behind the beach until the front forks had twisted. Although there was no proof, the Police pointed us in the direction of a gang of local lads they thought were responsible for the theft. They hung out in one of the portside bars and ran about on little mini-bikes which were regularly parked in a row along the quayside close to the water's edge.

That afternoon we went for a stroll down to the port and, low and behold there were the little bikes all neatly lined up just where we had expected to find them. There was a beer delivery lorry parked between the bar and the bikes blocking the view, so that no one could see us or the bikes. I don't need to spell out what happened next, but salt water can do terrible things to a motorbike. It didn't pay for the repair to the Yamaha, but it felt mighty good. A couple of days later I bumped into our friendly local Police officers who said, 'Did you hear about the big wave at the harbour at the weekend? What a shame, it swept all those lovely little bikes into the harbour,' and that was the end of that.

The standard of sport in the Regiment has always been exceptionally high. Fierce competition between the companies in all sports was encouraged and regular sports competitions were held. This was reflected nationally where members of the Regiment were national champions in both military and civilian events. Several members of the Regiment also represented the Legion when they won the Military World Team Cross-Country Championships.

In the late 1980s and through the early 1990s, we had a great champion by the name of Caporal Chef Steve Tunstall. Steve was both the national military and civilian cross-country champion. He was English but took French citizenship to enable himself to represent France in the World Cross-Country Championships in New Zealand. He finished an honourable eleventh with only runners from the African nations beating him to the line. After leaving the Legion he returned to the UK and regained his UK nationality, before becoming British cross-country champion in 1993 and 1994.

I had a particular interest in orienteering, qualifying as a military instructor in the discipline. I also ran cross-country for the Regiment in the veteran class and took part in national military competitions. Although I never won anything other than the regimental title, I enjoyed taking part.

We had superb facilities including a six-lane tartan track, a football/rugby pitch and a 50-metre swimming pool with a cover like a polytunnel that could be rolled back in the summer. There were three tennis courts and an outdoors shooting range. On top of all that, the gymnasium was big enough to hold two tennis courts and there was a separate, well-equipped weights gym. There was also the 'Centre Amphibie' on the beach, which was part of 3rd Company. There was cycling, rugby, football, orienteering, clay pigeon shooting, judo, martial arts, boxing and even a couple of microlight aircraft. At the Centre Amphibie instruction was available in sailing, canoeing, surfing and diving, while even skiing was available in the winter at 2nd Company's own centre in the mountains at Vergio. Several of the clubs were open to those with families, but the largest club of all was the parachute club, which was only to be expected in a parachute regiment. The parachute club was in action every weekend throughout the year and several of my longer-serving colleagues had made thousands of jumps.

Training in the Regiment was non-stop and, with each company having its own speciality, there was no room for anyone not prepared to give 100 per cent. There was a lot of effort put into being, or striving to be, the best in the world at what we did. Everyone wore their uniform and regimental badge with pride.

On a personal level I was still using my artistic abilities outside the office. Military subjects have always been a source of inspiration for an artist and I was no different. I painted several large murals on the interior walls of the different companies depicting their specialist activities.

Every year there was a national military art competition, with the winners of each military region taking part in the final held in Paris. The first year I entered I submitted a couple of watercolours depicting Corsican landscapes. Although they were well thought of I was advised by an experienced official military artist that to win such a competition you had to catch the eye of the judges by submitting something that was a bit controversial.

The following year I prepared a couple of paintings with the title 'The Price of Liberty'. They depicted an Afghan boy of twelve in one and his grandfather in the other, both of whom were prepared to give their lives in the fight against the Russian occupation of their country. Controversial they certainly were, I won the regional watercolour category and was invited to take part in the finals in Paris. The final was held each year in 'l'Orangerie du Senat', which is at the back of the French Parliament building. The competition was open to all military personnel, which in France includes the Gendarmerie, and the Fire and Ambulance services. That is in addition to the Army, Navy and Airforce. Originally there were thousands of contestants so it was a great honour to be in the final selection.

A panel of judges was drawn from senior officers from each service and the opening of the exhibition was performed by the President, Francois Mitterrand. My paintings caused quite a stir and the very person who had advised me to paint something controversial was the first to object to them being hung. In the end they were hung and I won first prize in the watercolour category. I was later approached by an Afghanistan Embassy official who offered me a very good price for them but was advised by, let's say, a French government official, not to go through with the sale. I still have them.

Having enjoyed my five minutes of fame in Paris, it was back to work as usual. A typical day started with getting up at 5.30 am, then off to the camp after breakfast. Each company assembled at 7.00 am, followed by an hour of collective physical activity which would normally be an 8-10k cross-country run with a quick swim in the sea if time permitted. You then had half an hour to have a shower and a coffee before starting the day's work at 8.30. Lunch was from 12.30 to 2.00 pm during which time I normally had a game of snooker in the mess before returning to work until 6.00 pm. If it was a jump day, it would be straight to the airport at 7.00 am, get in a couple of jumps then resume the normal day's work schedule. If you were on 24-hour guard duties, the changeover took place at 6.00 am each morning. When you came off duty at 6.00 the following morning, you had until 9.00 am to have a shower, breakfast and be back at your desk. It made for a long day, but everyone had to take their turn. As Chef du Post (NCO in charge of the guard), you only had guard duty half a dozen times a year. At 6.00 pm every night, an additional detail of eight Legionnaires made up the numbers for the night guard.

Every moment of the day was put to good use and the four front-line combat companies trained non-stop perfecting their specialist techniques. During my time with 1st Company, we had the use of an abandoned holiday camp close to the beach that we used for urban warfare training and was ideal for house-to-house combat.

The citadel in Calvi housed the Officers' Mess in what had been the Genoese governor's palace in the days when the island was occupied by the Italians. The father of Christopher Columbus was the Governor of Calvi for many years so Corsicans like to claim that as Columbus was born in Calvi he was therefore Corsican. He certainly would have spent much of his childhood there and there's a plaque in the citadel which acclaims this as fact.

The citadel also housed the old military hospital and it had been converted by the Legion to provide holiday accommodation for the first-year legionnaires who were not allowed to leave the island. It could also be used by legionnaires who had short-term leave and did not want to spend it in the camp. I used it a couple of times myself in my early days. The old hospital wards were converted to be used as club rooms by families for clubs such as painting, tapestry and embroidery.

The citadel, with its 100-foot-high ramparts, narrow streets and large stone buildings, was the ideal place to hold exercises. The four combat companies worked together in a demonstration of modern combat techniques. 3rd Company brought everyone involved in the assault across the bay onto the rocks below the ramparts, by Zodiac. 2nd Company then scaled the walls and set up ladders and ropes for the others to climb up. Once over the walls 1st Company would secure the area before the 4th Company would clear the area of any mines or booby traps. Once the citadel was secure the CRAP would make a helicopter assault onto the roof of the old hospital before working their way downwards into the building, using the stairs or by abseiling in through the windows to release the hostages. All of this was done in full view of the tourists who were still walking round the streets or visiting the cathedral. Once they were assured that it was only an exercise, they loved it and it always drew a large crowd. They cheered and applauded as the hostages were led out.

The spectacle did not stop there. Almost everyone left the way they had arrived but 2nd Company always concluded the show by making a spectacular death slide from the top of the ramparts into the public car park on the outside of the citadel. The finale was when the youngest member of the Company was strapped to a stretcher and lowered head first and at great speed into the car park. The stretcher was always rigged in such a way that it turned upside – a very scary moment for the youngster who had no idea what he was being set up for.

The 2nd Company had their own training camp in the mountains at Vergio, where they have excellent cold-weather conditions in winter for skiing and all aspects of mountain warfare. 3rd Company had their own amphibious training centre on the beach and train regularly with the French Navy using submarines and amphibious assault craft. 4th Company specialized in the use of explosives, mines and the use of snipers. They had two firing ranges at their disposal a short distance from the camp, the legionnaires training non-stop to become experts in their chosen specialities.

The heavy support company, 'Le Compagnie d'Eclairage et Appui', or CEA, had heavy and light mortar sections, 20mm anti-aircraft guns and other heavy equipment. All weapons and equipment used by the Regiment had to be transportable by parachute or support helicopters. Speed of deployment and withdrawal are so important on live-firing exercises that they trained regularly against the clock. The CRAP, although an autonomous specialist commando unit, came under the command of the CEA.

Since my retirement, two additional support companies have been added, plus a reserve company made up entirely of ex-legionnaires who live in and around Calvi. They perform non-combat duties such as manning the Regiment's fire service in the dry summer months when there are regular large wildfires on the island.

The Regiment regularly took part in joint exercises with the US Mediterranean Fleet so my translator skills were called on to liaise between the US commanders and the French High Command. On one such occasion we held a joint exercise in the south of Corsica. The US forces were making an amphibious landing with all the logistical might of the US Fleet. The REP was there to oppose the landings. We watched from a vantage point as the US Navy Seals landed and made the beach secure before calling in the main force which had remained out of sight several miles off the coast. There was no sign of any resistance and the beach master made the call for the invasion to start.

The sight that followed would have scared the life out of me if this had been for real. Out of the early morning mist came a wave of rapid assault craft of all shapes and sizes. From hovercraft carrying light assault vehicles to amphibious personnel carriers which suddenly roared up onto the beach to take up positions where they could put down covering fire to protect the arrival of the main force.

There is no doubt that the logistical military power of the US is awesome – way, way beyond anything that the European armies, or anyone else for that matter, can put together. Impressive as it was, logistics don't win wars. Within a couple of hours the beach was crawling with men and their equipment ready for the final push inland. But despite this impressive display, within minutes the small force from the REP had them pinned down on the beach. There was only one track out of the beach area and the best tanks and APCs could not cope with the Corsican terrain.

There were only 200 legionnaires facing the might of the US, but they had prepared their ambushes well and quickly disabled the leading tanks which then blocked the only exit from the beachhead. In all fairness, if this had been the real thing, the US attack helicopters and fighter aircraft would have made short work of any resistance on the ground. Nevertheless, it was a lesson worth learning for everyone involved. The REP then made a tactical withdrawal and the American staff officers were impressed by the tactics, efficiency and mobility of the unit. Independent judges decided what had been hit or disabled and there was no arguing with them. If they said that you were dead, that was it, you were withdrawn from the exercise and couldn't turn up somewhere else.

The next phase of the exercise was to take place at an airfield on the other side of the island. As we drove to the location we came across a regular French army tank unit manning a roadblock. They were equipped with AMX 10RC six-wheeled light tanks which the Americans had never seen. There were six jeeps and a minibus in our convoy and although we were displaying observer markings, I expected some kind of reaction from the French unit as we pulled up in front of them. Instructed to tell the tank commander to present his unit to the Americans, I walked across to the lead tank and signalled for him to come out. Nothing. I climbed onto the nearest tank and noticed that the hatch was slightly ajar. By now there was a row of generals and their staff officers in front of the tank, waiting. I pulled the hatch up and instead of receiving a mouthful of abuse, all I heard was the sound of . . . zzzz . . . zzzz . . . zzzz! The entire crew were sound asleep in the warmth of their tank.

By now some of the other crews had become aware of our presence and hatches were popping open on all the other tanks. Someone must have said something over their command link because the commander suddenly shot out of the hatch like a jack-in-the-box. There were some red faces and I thought that the French generals were going to explode. The presentation was made and the Americans were impressed by the vehicle, if not the crew commander. I was sure that the career of the officer in command had just suddenly come to a halt. We continued on our way to the airport leaving the poor sod contemplating his future in the military.

The scenario at the airport was that a group of terrorists had taken over the control tower and were holding civilian hostages. There were to be no negotiations and this was to be a demonstration by an American Special Forces unit of how to overpower the terrorists without loss of life. What happened next was as impressive as the beach landing had been. Two Hercules C130 transports were on final approach and covering fire was being supplied by Cobra attack helicopters. The idea was to keep all of the terrorists indoors and under cover while the Hercs landed. Their firepower was simulated by lazers and computers registered the imaginary impacts. So far so good.

Within minutes the leading Herc touched down but kept rolling with its nose wheel well off the ground. The ramp at the rear was down and had been adapted to run along the surface of the runway on small wheels. Three armoured cars rolled backwards down the ramp out of the moving aircraft but as soon as they were on the tarmac, a forward gear was engaged and they fanned out to provide ground cover for the second aircraft which was now performing the same manoeuvre.

The leading Herc had raised its ramp and was now lifting off at the other end of the runway as three more jeeps backed out of the second aircraft. I had heard of this tactic before but had never seen it done. It had taken less than two minutes to get the six vehicles and their crews into the airport ready to mount the ground attack. The Hercs were now circling the airport awaiting the all clear to land and recover the teams and the hostages. The Cobra gunships were still flying low over the area to provide instant firepower should it be required.

Within minutes of landing the terminal building was secure and it was confirmed that the hostages were being held in the control tower. The problem they faced was that they were being held five floors up and because of the time it would have taken to mount a conventional assault, the hostages would be dead. One of the Americans spoke remarkably good French and so an audacious plan was hatched. Terrorists in real life like publicity for their cause and are not adverse to appearing on TV so he simply pressed the intercom button on the door and said that he was from a TV news crew who were there to interview them. After a minute or so, the door buzzed and was opened by one of the guys acting as a terrorist. He was quickly overpowered, the assault team were up the stairs and into the control room in a flash. A stun grenade was let off causing everyone without ear protection to drop to their knees holding their heads in shock. Everyone was made to lie on the floor and had their hands tagged. There and then was not the time to decide who were terrorists and who were hostages, thereby reducing the chance of confusion in the heat of the moment.

Everyone was led downstairs where they were searched to sort out the goodies from the baddies. During all of this the two Hercs had landed and had taxied back to the end of the runway. The hostages were released and the terrorists bundled into one of the jeeps while the release team piled into the other five before they roared off in the direction of the Hercs and drove straight in. The tail gates closed and the Hercs were roaring down the runway with the Cobras in close formation behind them. It was so impressive.

When I looked at my watch it showed that the whole thing from landing to take-off had taken exactly twenty-three minutes. I'm sure that if it had been the real thing, having a film crew on the spot would have appealed to the ego of the terrorists and they would have reacted in exactly the same way. The important thing about joint exercises like this is not who wins, but what you learn from them.

The Legion uses an interesting obstacle course just outside Bonifacio in the very south of the island. It is not the hardest course in the world but it requires a little bit of courage to complete. Some of the US Marines wanted to give it a go but their officers were a bit worried about litigation if there was an injury. In the end a compromise was reached and it was agreed that they would 'walk' the course. If any of them didn't want to do a particular obstacle then they wouldn't be forced. Many of them said that it was one of the best things they had ever done. A team from the REP demonstrated how it should be done and won a great cheer and applause from the Americans.

The world is an ever-changing place and all the training in the world can't prepare you for the real thing. With the ending of the cold war and the fall of the Berlin Wall, everything has changed in this troubled world of ours. When Saddam invaded Kuwait it brought to an end all attempts at holding the reins on the troubled Middle East. It was just the start of all the turbulent times we are experiencing today.

Up until that time most conflicts smouldering around the world had been internal affairs such as the UK's problems in Northern Ireland, and to some extent the Falklands War. At least there we were fighting an enemy we understood and had a good idea where they were coming from politically, even if we didn't agree. What was about to happen was a completely new ball game. When Saddam made his move on Kuwait, the reaction of the Western powers was instant. It came as a complete surprise to everyone except the Intelligence agencies who had been trying to warn the politicians for years that we were facing a huge threat in the form of a new breed of extreme fundamentalist terrorism based in the Middle East.

As ever, the politicians were afraid to inform the general public of the dangers we were facing. Perhaps it was because they didn't want to damage their own little empires by being the bearers of bad news. The lack of response to what was happening in the Middle East was interpreted by extremist governments and terror groups as a weakness to be exploited, leading us to the shambles we all are now experiencing.

CHAPTER 11

The Day When All of our Lives Changed

Because of the threat of imminent war in the Gulf, France went to the UN Security Council and asked that the Legion be recognized as an official part of the French Army. This was a monumental moment in the history of the French Foreign Legion. Its status had changed for ever.

Within days of this request being accepted, the Legion started to deploy units to the Gulf ahead of the Regular French Army units. The 1st Cavalry Regiment, the 2nd Infantry Regiment plus a detachment from the 6th Engineer Regiment left for Saudi Arabia to join the Coalition forces forming up to repulse Saddam's army, which was occupying Kuwait. All the CRAP units of the French 11th Parachute Division were also put on alert for immediate deployment. This would be a mechanized war which meant that parachute units like the REP would not be involved directly in the conflict. It would be a different story if it came down to having to move into cities like Baghdad, but for the moment, as a regiment, we would not be involved.

On the day word came that the CRAP were to be deployed to the Gulf, we were on exercise in mainland France. Within hours we had flown back to Calvi, packed our gear and were heading back to join the other CRAP units.

On arrival in Saudi Arabia, it was decided that the Special Force units should be multi-national, drawing on the best expertise available from within the Coalition forces. We had arrived weeks ahead of the principal forces. Heavy equipment had to be brought in from the four corners of the world and it would be at least a couple of months before Coalition forces would be ready to move. We had arrived early with the intention of making sorties into Iraq to gather information about the deployment and strength of the Iraqi forces remaining in the country, either in reserve for Kuwait, or as protection for the Iraqi military infrastructure such as air bases and ammunition supply dumps. Satellite images could tell you a lot but this information still requires to be confirmed by good old-fashioned ground work.

Saddam had made a bold move and I am sure that he did not believe that the UN would sanction the use of force to remove him from Kuwait. It was his belief that if the West became aggressive towards him, the Arab world would unite to back him in a holy war. This was the first of many errors of judgement to be made by Saddam.

We were on strict instructions to avoid all contact with the enemy during the build-up. It was clear from the information we gathered in our sorties into Iraq that their forces were stretched to the limit and did not have the capacity to take on the huge force that was building up on the other side of the border. The Republican Guard were the only professional soldiers in Saddam's army and had been used for the invasion of Kuwait. Although his army was large in numbers, it was made up of young untrained conscripts who didn't appear to be aware of what was about to descend on them from a great height.

One thing that did worry us was the large numbers of mobile Scud missile units that could be deployed. Israel and Saudi Arabia were well within striking distance and we believed that they could be equipped with chemical warheads. The fact that they could be disguised as container lorries made them hard to track from the air.

I had brought the new digital photographic equipment with me which enabled me to send back real-time images of anti-aircraft defences and their exact location using GPS. This was modern warfare. The GPS location of a designated target would be fed into the guidance system of a missile which would then take it out even if it could not be seen from the air.

In the middle of all this we were suddenly redeployed. We were preparing for another mission into Iraq when we were told to grab all our gear and get on a Hercules. We had no idea where we were heading until we were halfway into the flight. The pro-French government in Tchad had suddenly been overthrown in a military coup backed by Libya. Everyone's attention was focused on what was happening in the Middle East and I suppose they thought that the coup would be unopposed. What they'd failed to appreciate was that French parachute regiments would not only be available but were on G1 alert and could respond immediately. France would not intervene in the internal affairs of the country, but was committed to the protection of the expat community and to ensure that no third party crossed the borders of Tchad or played a part in the disruption of the democratic process of the country.

The airport at Ndjemina was already under the control of the French forces stationed in the country, so our arrival was not a problem. The Regiment flew out from Calvi and arrived just fifteen minutes after our own arrival. Our immediate mission was to secure the safety of all foreigners and escort them to the airport. We could not force them to leave, but few were willing to risk their lives in what was a very hostile and fragile environment.

Groups of Tchadien soldiers were roaming the streets, no one seemed to be in charge and most were under the influence of alcohol or drugs. They were looting the shops and generally terrorizing anyone they came across – it was not a place to be white or living in an isolated villa.

Two Air France 747s were brought in to assist with the rapid evacuation of the civilians who were now packing the airport. Many had lived and worked in Tchad for years and were leaving behind their jobs, homes and in some cases everything they possessed. There was no guarantee that they would ever be able to return. I felt sorry for many of them. There were also those, mostly businessmen I might add, who were trying everything to get to the head of the queue to get on the aircraft. They soon found themselves at the back of the queue again when they were hauled out of the line by the legionnaires in charge of boarding the aircraft.

At the front of the terminal there were hundreds of 4x4 Toyota Landcruisers abandoned with the keys still in the ignitions. Several were commandeered by ourselves for transport and I managed to get my hands on a top-of-the-range model left by a very obnoxious gentleman. This particular vehicle was eventually given to someone who had once been part of the Regiment and now ran an orphanage just outside the capital with the aid of the REP and families, who regularly collected clothes and books to send out to him. There was no way he would abandon the children and the Regiment left a combat group with him to ensure their security. By the evening of the third day all the civilians who wished to leave had been evacuated. There had been some nervous moments but the evacuation had gone well. Not a single shot had been exchanged and things were a lot quieter in the town center.

Things changed suddenly when two giant Ilyushin IL-76 transport aircraft belonging to the Libyan Air Force flew across the border on a direct course for Ndjemina. Two French Mirage fighters were scrambled and we were told by the new government that they had permission to land. A delegation from the new Tchadien government arrived at the airport insisting that they should be given access to the aircraft when they landed. They claimed that the aircraft were there to pick up hundreds of Libyan prisoners who were being held in Tchad and were to be repatriated to Libya. Permission was given for the aircraft to land, but they were directed to a parking spot chosen by us and a security cordon was thrown round the aircraft. No one was allowed to disembark and we escorted two representatives of the Tchadien government onto the aircraft.

Lorries arrived carrying over 300 prisoners in prison uniforms that looked to me to be no more than striped pyjamas. Most were infirm and malnourished, and it was clear that they had not had an easy time. I wondered how many had died and why the French authorities and the Red Cross claimed not to have known of their existence. They were brought into the airport and lined up between the terminal and the waiting aircraft. We did our best to ensure that they were all Libyans as claimed and not Tchadiens from the old regime being flown out to Libya. While this was taking place, two armoured Mercedes limos were rolled out of the aircraft onto the tarmac. It was claimed that they were gifts from Colonel Gadaffi to the new Tchadien President. Closer examination showed that they were filled with gifts and ladies' clothes, including fur coats. The cars were seized by the French authorities and secured in an aircraft hangar within the French military air base at the other side of the airport.

The aircraft left an hour later with their human cargo and the following morning the same two aircraft were back on the tarmac for a repeat operation, although this time minus the gifts.

Before this exchange of prisoners could take place, a couple of 'men in black suits', came into the airport and asked to speak to our Colonel. They were accompanied by the French Ambassador and the American Consul. Not all of the Libyan prisoners captured over the years had found their way into the hands of the Tchadiens. A large number had been taken to a special detention camp at a secret location about 50 miles outside of the capital. The men in black suits said that the Tchadien government did not know anything about the existence of the camp, or of its prisoners. The French Ambassador claimed that the first he had heard of it was an hour earlier.

The camp was run by the CIA and was used to train those in detention to go back into their own country to undermine the Gadaffi regime, commit acts of sabotage, assassinations and to spy for the Americans. All of this was done for financial reward and the promise of a new life in the States on completion of their missions. Due to the new pro Libyan government, the existence of the camp was not now sustainable and they wanted to fly their prisoners out of the country. Everything had to be done in the utmost secrecy and a plan was made to bring them to the airport and fly them out without the Tchadiens or Libyans knowing what was going on.

The problem was that we were going to have both Libyan and American aircraft at the airport at the same time. At 2.00 pm exactly, two US Galaxy C-5B transporters landed, we closed the airport down and confined the Libyans to their aircraft. When they saw the American aircraft touch down they were worried that they were about to mount an assault on them, but the aircraft continued to the far end of the runway before coming to a halt in a position out of sight of the terminal. The prisoners were transported in covered lorries to a point just outside the boundary fence next to where the American planes were waiting. Two French helicopters circled low overhead causing a sandstorm with the downdraft of their rotor blades, effectively preventing anyone seeing what was going on. We cut a hole in the fence and quickly loaded the prisoners onto the aircraft. The whole operation took less than fifteen minutes from touchdown to take-off, and the CIA left with them.

Just before they left they gave us the coordinates and keys for another secret location. They did not tell us what we would find there but asked us to destroy everything. Less than five minutes from the airport we found five large brick warehouses enclosed by a 10-foot-high barbed-wire security fence. There were two civilian articulated lorries parked inside the compound and the sign on the gate said that it was a transport company. We had passed this complex many times and had not given it a second glance.

There was no one about and the padlocks looked brand new – not a problem as we had the keys. When we went inside the buildings we found a complete arsenal, enough weapons to equip an army. The strange thing was that although many of the weapons seemed to be of Russian or Chinese origin, they weren't. Closer examination showed that the AK47 assault rifles were of American manufacture and were still wrapped in their original packaging. We also found a large quantity of American and French-made ground-to-air missiles, mines, grenades, explosives and thousands of rounds of small-arms munitions. When we searched the offices we found lots of paperwork that clearly indicated where the munitions came from.

Our orders were to destroy everything we found, including the paperwork. In the last warehouse we found a perfectly preserved ex-Soviet helicopter gunship. It had all of the identity marks removed and looked as though it was about to have a paint job. It had all its armaments in place with air-to-surface missiles hanging from its stubby little wings. Where on earth had this come from?

A short time later, the two Merc limos were driven into the complex and secured in one of the warehouses, still with the 'gifts' inside them. We rigged the entire complex with explosives and withdrew to a safe distance. An area of approximately one square mile had been secured round the complex for safety reasons. When the explosives were fired, the resulting detonations were seen and heard for miles. The ground shook and a huge fireball climbed into the sky.

The Tchadien authorities demanded an explanation as to what had happened but were told that the warehouse complex must have been destroyed by a stray round. The odd mortar bomb had landed near the airport and the explanation was feasible. It didn't explain what had been in the buildings to cause such a huge detonation but it was the best they were going to get. After the departure of the American aircraft, the transfer of the second batch of Libyans held by the Tchadiens went ahead without a hitch.

There was an unspoken agreement amongst all of the parties involved that no questions would be asked and the incident was closed. We never found out where the Americans had flown their prisoners to, but perhaps it was the first example of American rendition flights. We had done nothing to aid or hinder the political changes taking place within Tchad but we had cut off all physical links between Libya and the would-be government. Without this aid, the revolt was short lived.

The Regiment maintained its presence in the country for a few weeks but we headed back to Saudi Arabia where things were hotting up as the Coalition forces grew in size ready for the push to remove the Iraqi forces from Kuwait.

CHAPTER 12

Operation Desert Storm

The American, British and French heavy tanks and artillery had arrived and were ready for deployment in the first part of the offensive now known to the world as 'Desert Storm', or as 'Operation Daguet' by the French. Huge military camps had sprung up all over Saudi Arabia and it was clear to us that this very large army was far greater in size than was required simply to eject the Iraqi forces from Kuwait. Even more impressive was the air power. I had never seen so many helicopters – they were everywhere, ferrying personnel, freight and heavy guns forward to the more advanced positions. At times it looked as if they were moving loads from A to B and back again. Perhaps this was a planned exercise to confuse any spies watching the build-up. It confused us. It seemed to be a logistical nightmare but the amazing thing was that if you asked for something, you got it.

When the Legion tank regiment eventually arrived by sea, they were immediately deployed on the Saudi-Iraq border. We also noted that the American main battle tanks, the Abrams M1, were kept on the back of their transporters.

Because we had been redeployed to Tchad, we had not been included in the plans for the approaching invasion and the recon units had been restructured to work without us. As it turned out, this was good news for us as it meant that we would stay together as a unit and would be working in our normal combat groups. It was always good to know that you could trust and rely on the rest of your team if things got a bit heavy. Being the Legion we had our own linguists and every speciality we might need. When the air strikes started we knew that the ground hostilities would not be long in starting. Wave after wave of fighter bombers left on air strikes every day, striking at targets designated by units like our own.

At 7.19 am on 23 February 1991, we crossed the border into Iraq well to the north and west of Kuwait, along with 4th Company of the 2nd Legion Infantry Regiment (2eme REI). We were fully equipped for chemical warfare and dressed in full NBC combat gear. The actual invasion of Iraq was led by the 1st Legion Cavalry Regiment (1er REC), quickly

Parachuting into Camp Raffalli on a clear winter's day.

Freefall above Corsica
taken from a helmet
camera at about 2,500m.

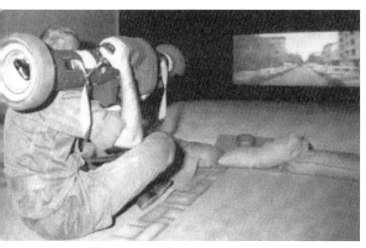

The indoor Cini-tir range
being used for anti-tank
weapon training.

Above the camp and Calvi.

A watercolour showing the activities of the 3rd Company.

A series of pen-and-ink drawings I did showing the speciality of each company: 1st Company (Commando); 2nd Company (Mountain Warfare); 3rd Company (Amphibious Warfare).

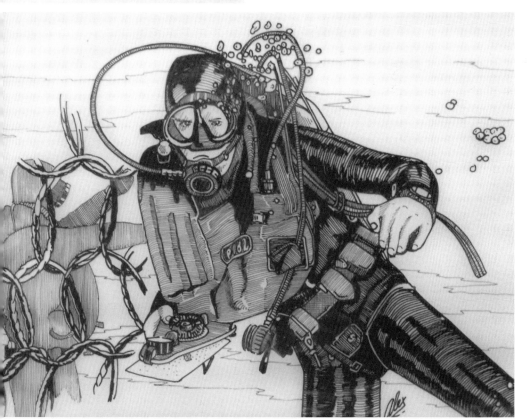

CEA (Compagnie Eclairage et Apuis) – Heavy Support Company.

CCS (Compagnie Commandement et Service)) – Command & Support Company (Administration, medics, mechanics, stores, mess facilities etc.).

etting ready to jump at Calvi.

cks don't work in the desert.

First Gulf War – US Forces with oil well fires in the background.

First Gulf War – deep behind enemy lines in Iraq.

First Gulf War – taking cover for the night in Iraq.

The author working on maps and plans of Sarajevo just before the Regiment's deployment there.

y office in Sarajevo.

Sarajevo – south of the airport (Bosnian side of the road).

Sarajevo – Serbian side south of the airport, southern entrance.

enches just outside the airport at Sarajevo.

e tunnel under the airport runway dug by the Bosnians (1993).

At −20°C even the camera had to be protected against the cold.

General Ratko Mladić (Serbian) arriving at Sarajevo Airport for peace talks (1993).

rajevo Airport.

rajevo 1993.

My small armoured car in the centre of Sarajevo – called a VBL (Véhicule Blindé Léger).

MINISTERE DE LA DEFENSE

RÉPUBLIQUE FRANÇAISE

ETAT-MAJOR DES ARMEES

Ordre Général n° 1036

CITATION

L'Amiral J. LANXADE
Chef d'Etat-Major des armées

VU   le décret n°56-371 du 11 avril 1956 modifié, portant création de la Croix de la Valeur
        Militaire,
VU   l'instruction n°19000/SD/CAB/DECO/F du 27 avril 1956 pour l'application de ce
        décret,
VU   la décision particulière n°22804 du 06 juillet 1992.

<u>C I T E</u>

à l'ordre de la Brigade

le Caporal-chef LOCHRIE Alexander - NI : 83 137 67846
2° Régiment Etranger de Parachutistes

> *"Engagé au sein du Bataillon d'Infanterie Français de SARAJEVO dans le cadre de la Force de Protection des Nations-Unies depuis le 13 janvier 1993, s'est particulièrement distingué le 19 janvier 1993 au cours d'une mission d'observation sur l'aéroport. Pris sous le feu direct d'un tireur isolé, a poursuivi malgré tout sa mission avec calme et détermination.*
> *Le 25 mars 1993 a été blessé au visage par de nombreux éclats de verre lors de la prise à partie du Poste de Commandement du bataillon par une arme automatique.*
> *Pour son attitude sous le feu, mérite d'être cité en exemple."*

<u>CETTE CITATION COMPORTE L'ATTRIBUTION DE LA CROIX DE LA VALEUR
MILITAIRE AVEC ETOILE DE BRONZE</u>

A PARIS, le   LE 15 AÓUT 1993

LANXADE

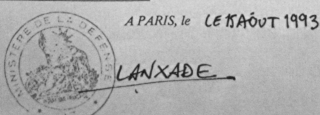

tation for my Military Cross.

Being awarded the Military Cross.

My medals: Military Cross with star (Sarajevo); Wounded in Action with star (Sarajevo); Overseas Mission (Tchad); UN Peacekeeping Medal; General Service Medal (silver).

Competition painting.

The author today.

followed by the main US armoured division spread out across the desert.

There was no opposition of any kind. Enemy positions were being carpet bombed ahead of us, reducing areas the size of two football fields to dust by the accuracy of the bombing. Artillery fire and ship-to-shore missiles fired from surface ships and submarines hundreds of miles away were striking targets with pinpoint accuracy. It was very impressive to us, but must have been terrifying if you were on the receiving end.

There is a popular belief that a cruise missile has the capacity to find its way through windows and down chimneys. This belief is something that has always been encouraged as it helps to spread fear amongst the enemy. It's not quite true – almost, but not quite. The on-board guidance system is incredibly accurate and the missiles have the ability to follow a three-dimensional guidance system at low level right to the target area. That in itself is a remarkable example of modern technology, but when it gets to its destination it requires some assistance from the ground to enhance its ability. To do this a system of target designation is used involving a team on the ground who guide the missile onto its target using a hand-held laser. The exact location of the team on the ground is sent to a control aircraft flying high over the target. This location is then fed to the on-board guidance system on the missile. Once locked on, the missile picks up the exact point of desired impact from the hand-held laser and that is exactly where it will impact, to the inch. It could be a window, a door, an aircraft, a truck or even a moving target.

The resistance was so weak that we had to leapfrog ahead of the main force to acquire targets for the aircraft and missiles we were undertaking missions further and further into Iraq. It was not long before the opposition realized that there had to be guidance teams on the ground calling in the air strikes, which meant that such missions were risky and guaranteed to get the old adrenaline going. Helicopters were used to put us in and sometimes they had to make some very hot extractions, but that was what we were trained for. Fighters were called in to cover our extraction by mission controllers in the command aircraft high above our heads.

Up until now I had still to fire my weapon in anger. Our biggest problem was proving to be the huge numbers of Iraqi soldiers wanting to give themselves up. We simply handed out leaflets in Arabic telling them that they should surrender to the main force which was only a couple of hours behind us. They were astonished when we drove off leaving them behind and most sat down in groups to await the arrival of the main force. Some even laid down their weapons and went home. Many were no more than boys and had no idea what was going on or even that they were at war.

We had no information about what was happening in Kuwait or anywhere else in the country. We had not been told to slow down so assumed that the same scenario was unfolding across the rest of Iraq. We had heard that some Scuds had been fired against Israel from the northwest but that was nowhere near our area of operation.

Our next objective was to attack a munitions depot in the region of As-Salam. We found lots of cluster bombs and several hundred tons of different types of munitions. The following day we reconnoitered an old fort just to the north of the munitions dump and were joined by another French unit who were going to install a command post in the fort. Disaster struck when two unexploded cluster bombs just outside the fort went off as a patrol was passing. Two men were killed and twenty-five injured. Unfortunately two of our own men were amongst the injured, one of them with a serious thigh injury. He was repatriated back to France but thankfully made a full recovery and was able to return to active service.

There was little or no resistance on the ground and any combat was very one sided. We were only involved in a couple of very brief firefights with retreating Iraqis. Not once did we come under direct attack. The American air power was devastating, as was clearly demonstrated by the attack on an Iraqi convoy trying to flee north from Kuwait. Only two aircraft made the attack, destroying over 150 vehicles in one pass.

Resistance was so poor that we found ourselves just short of Baghdad waiting for the main force to play catch-up. We were told to halt where we were and await instructions. On 9 March the order was given to pull out and to return to Saudi Arabia. No reason was given and we were not in a position to ask. Operation Desert Storm was over. From crossing the frontier into Iraq to our withdrawal back to our jump-off point had taken just two weeks.

There was one serious outcome that arose from our rapid withdrawal. We had found some ammunition dumps hidden in huge underground complexes which we had come across by accident. We knew that there were dozens more that we had not found, but because of the risk of chemical contamination, we were not allowed to blow them up. We were told to note the location and report what we had found to the experts who would deal with them at a later date. The problem was that all of the Coalition forces withdrew from Iraq so quickly that no one ever got back to them. Years later when the UN inspectors went back into Iraq they either didn't have details of the locations or when they did examine the sites there was nothing there.

If you believe anything that Saddam said, then the Iraqis' destroyed them. I don't and neither does anyone else who saw what we had left behind. Saddam did not believe until the day it happened that he would be deposed, so why would he destroy what he thought of as his ace card – a huge store of chemical weapons. If they are not still lying out there, then where are they? That is a question that worries me. He would rather have passed them into the hands of his worst Arab enemies than destroy them or let anyone from the West or UN inspectors find them. So where and when will they turn up? If, God forbid, they ever find their way into the hands of terrorists, we will all pay the price for the huge mistake made not only by the politicians, but by everyone who called out for an end to hostilities before the job was done properly. These are the same people who today shout about the human rights of those who show no respect for the rights of anyone. Those who die at the hands of the terrorist have no rights, but still they cry foul if they are as much as stopped and asked to prove their identity.

There was one interesting little episode which was experienced by the Regiment when it flew back to France after the intervention in Tchad. Although the story was told to me by a senior officer in the Regiment, I have no reason to disbelieve it. The Air France 747 bringing part of the Regiment back to Corsica after the intervention in Tchad was diverted to Marseille. What happened next, although it had an amusing ending, was nevertheless a scandal and insult to the integrity of the Regiment. On the order of the French Secret Service (the DST), the aircraft was directed to a remote part of the airport normally designated for anti-hijacking operations, where it was surrounded by armed gendarmes who escorted everyone off the plane and onto buses. They were then taken to a part of the main terminal that had been closed off to the public. Personal baggage was taken off the aircraft and brought to the terminal to be searched. The gendarmes said that they had been instructed to search for weapons, explosives and 'documents' that might have been brought back by the legionnaires as souvenirs from Tchad. The gendarmes were not happy about being given the task and went about it in a very half-hearted manner, passing the luggage through the scanners without really looking at the screens. There was some light relief when a sniffer dog went mad in front of a pack before diving into it to pull out a pair of very smelly socks – the pack belonged to the Colonel in Chief of the Regiment.

A short time later the Colonel of the gendarmes arrived and ordered his men to stop the search. He told the three agents from the DST that if they wished to do the search themselves then they should get on with it and apologized to our Colonel before withdrawing his men. There was no doubt in everyone's mind that the search had been asked for by the Americans to make sure that no incriminating documents had been brought back from Tchad which related to the munitions or anything else we might have found.

The aircraft was soon on its way again and it is the only time that a 747 has landed on the short runway at Calvi.

Our own return was uneventful other than we were given first-class service by the hostesses on the Air France chartered flight from Saudi Arabia back to France. It didn't feel like we had been in a war but it had been a great experience.

CHAPTER 13

A Touch of Normality

Although I had not experienced anything in the Gulf which I would call stressful, that does not mean that others didn't. I can only speak for myself and have not heard of any legionnaires suffering from 'Gulf War Syndrome'. We were certainly filled with a cocktail of drugs before we went out there, but personally I have not suffered any ill effects myself. Perhaps I am just one of the lucky ones as no doubt a combination of stress and prescribed drugs can have an effect on some people.

I also believe that the quality of training in the Legion goes a long way in the preparation of the individual to take part in real operations. It's not just the technical training, but psychological attitude. You can see it in the way that legionnaires conduct themselves, how they dress, and their overall professionalism and attitude when in a combat zone. There is just something that makes them stand out from the rest. Perhaps that's why they manage to get past the selection process in the first place.

I was certainly tired and ready for a break so was delighted when I was given a month's leave and intended to relax back home in Scotland this time. While at home on leave I met someone who was to come into my life and change it for ever. We had known each other for many years, although our lives had taken separate paths until then.

I headed back to Calvi at the end of my break with a new spring in my step. It was over seven years since I had had any kind of relationship, even casual. Work had occupied every moment of my day up until then and I can't say that I had any regrets about living on my own. I hadn't even given it a thought. I wasn't into one-night stands and have never paid for sex in my life, although I do believe that there is a place for well-controlled, legalized brothels. It takes sex off the street, protects the women physically and medically and satisfies a need for sexual release that might otherwise end up with a woman being raped or worse.

Once back in Calvi I started to communicate with my new-found love, sending and receiving a letter almost every day. This was in an age before the use of emails replaced good old-fashioned letters. You still can't beat a good old love letter, which is far more personal and romantic.

*

The next couple of months were spent getting back into the daily routine of the Regiment and achieving peak fitness. When you are involved in live operations you can't just pop out for a quick run. You have to get back quickly to the standard of fitness expected in the REP. It is the months of expending energy rather than building it up that takes its toll. I also had to take into account that I was now in my forties. Most people my age couldn't run the length of the street never mind carrying 30 kilos while in full combat gear.

I had learned a lot in the Gulf and had had the chance to use some very sophisticated equipment not normally available to us. Despite this, the most important lesson of all had been that a well-trained, fit, dedicated soldier is of more value than any of the fanciest pieces of modern technology. Without the first, the second is useless. The American war machine works on the opposite theory and is designed round equipment and logistical wizardry, but I had watched it all grind to a halt at times because the men on the ground were not up to the job required of them. It's not the fault of the men, it's the American principle of bigger is better and all the money goes on logistics. One very senior American officer once told me that there was so much money involved, and so many people from the politicians down taking their cut of the profits, that those who had to use the equipment had no say in its purchase.

In January 1992, I brought the new love of my life out to Corsica for a couple of weeks' holiday. The weather was beautiful and we had a wonderful time getting to know each other properly. I also enjoyed showing off this beautiful island. A couple of months later she moved to Calvi permanently. Having recently moved into a fabulous flat overlooking the port, with a glorious view across the bay to the camp and the mountains, I was now able to combine work with a normal home life and was back to my old level of fitness.

Saint Michel is the patron saint of parachutists. Yes, even the Legion has one, which is always an excuse for a bit of healthy competition between the companies. There is an intensive week of sporting activity, a big parade at the camp and an open day for the public with entertainment, side shows and of course a lot of parachuting.

On the day of the parade, there can be anything up to 2,000 people lining the parade square to watch as the regimental colour is escorted from the museum and paraded before the assembled troops. As many as a hundred 'Anciens' – members of the ex-Legionnaires Association – march behind their own colour and pass in front of the Regiment to take their place in the celebrations. They are all dressed in a green beret with the REP badge, white shirt and green tie, black blazer, grey trousers and black shoes. They march with pride and are loudly applauded by the crowd which is made up of families, local Corsicans and tourists who have flocked to see this legendary regiment. Once everyone is assembled there is usually a fly-past by several Hercules and Transall transport aircraft, quickly followed by 'La Patrouille de France', the French equivalent of the 'Red Arrows' aerobatic display team.

You have to watch a Legion parade to appreciate it. There is no comparison between the sharp precision of the British Army and the slow swagger of the Legion. It is quite different but equally good to watch. Everyone has a great time at 'Saint Michel'. The kids love getting their hands on real boys' toys, sliding down a rope from the top of the jump tower, and taking part in all the sideshows. The highlight of the day is the display by the aerobatic aircraft followed by demonstrations of both fixed and free-fall parachuting. One of the free-fall teams always makes a spectacular landing in the middle of the parade square which never fails to excite the crowd. It's a great public relations exercise and the crowds seem to get bigger every year.

The ultimate parade in France is the one that takes place in Paris on 14 July every year – Bastille Day. A different Legion regiment takes part every year and parades behind the Legion's own band from Aubagne, 'La Musique Principal'. Because of the slow marching pace of the Legion, they always go last just before the mechanized part of the parade. All of the regiments taking part march twenty abreast down the Champs-Elysées. When they get to the point where the President takes the salute, they divide, ten to the right, ten to the left. By tradition, the Legion divides for no one, not even the President, and the whole regiment goes to the President's right. They are the only regiment to do this. Experiencing the fervour of the crowd is something that I will never forget. I was not taking part in the parade but walking down the inside of the barriers taking the official photographs for the Regiment.

After the parade, a certain number from each regiment dine at the Presidential Palace or at the Mayor's reception. I was honoured to be sent to dine with the Mayor, who at that time was Jacques Chirac. By pure chance I found myself seated next to him, and enjoyed his company and conversation throughout the meal. He seemed to like the Legion and asked me what hall of the Mairie the others were in. We then went to find them and he spent the next half an hour in our company singing Legion songs, all of which he knew. That night we were free to go out in town and it was impossible to buy a drink or pay for your meal. As soon as they saw the Legion uniform, that was it. We had a night to remember and a sore head in the morning to go with it.

Corsica is a huge piece of granite that was pushed up out of the sea at the time when the Alps were created. When you look at a map, you see that the island is in perfect alignment with the Alps and the mountainous areas are as rugged as anything you find on the Continent. France has a series of classified walks in the Alps and the Pyrenees, but the most difficult one is the GR20 in Corsica. These walks, or 'Grand Randonnées', border on serious mountain climbing and should not be undertaken by anyone inexperienced.

Every year, each company completes the GR20 which follows the mountainous spine of Corsica over a route that goes from sea level, over valleys and through mountain passes. It takes you through 110-foot-high pine forests, past mountain lakes and high plateaux. The scenery is spectacular. The highlight of the walk is standing on top of Corsica's highest mountain, Monti Cinto. At roughly 9,000 feet it is twice the height of Ben Nevis, the highest mountain in the UK.

When standing on the top, you can see the length and breadth of the island, and on a clear day all the way to the French and Italian coasts, and beyond to the snow-capped Alps. It is a route of exceptional natural beauty but requires a degree of experience to negotiate some of the passes. 'La Col de Solitude' or 'Lonely Pass' is an example. The risk level here is such that a permanent security system has been fixed into the rock face. You have to negotiate a curve in the rock face walking on a ledge which is no more than a foot wide, with a drop into the gorge below of over 500 feet. You can't see round the curve and it is an irresponsible person who tries to get round the ledge without using the safety system. Before starting out you have to shout out in case there is someone coming the other way. Even hooked up it is quite daunting. You need to face the rock and you have the feeling that the weight of your pack will pull you off the ledge. Quite a few ramblers have had to turn back at this point because one or more of their party have refused to negotiate the hazard.

Being the regimental photographer, each company requested my presence on their walk and most of the legionnaires wanted a souvenir photograph of themselves doing the GR20. This meant that during my eight years as regimental photographer, I completed the GR20 seventeen times. Sometimes two companies would set out from opposite ends of the route. I would set out with one company and change over when they met in the middle. Although it was hard going it was always a pleasure.

If you are into serious hill walking I strongly recommend you go to Corsica and walk the GR20. You won't regret it and will probably come back for more.

Mountains are never the same twice and I completed the walk in all weathers. The GR20 is undertaken by thousands of civilians every year. Many forget that even if Corsica is in the middle of the Mediterranean, weather conditions in the mountains can change at a moment's notice. Every year without fail, the mountain rescue teams have to go up and rescue some idiot at over 3,000ft caught out in a storm and freezing conditions, wearing nothing more than shorts and a tee shirt.

For us holidays never last for long. World events were on the move again, and so were we.

CHAPTER 14

Why are We Here and What are We Doing?

The next few chapters have been the hardest part of my story to write, and I don't hesitate to say that the operation I am about to describe was to change my way of looking at world events, and to question the motives of those who make decisions that change, even destroy, the lives of millions.

The mission given to the Regiment by the UN was to maintain the security of Sarajevo Airport during the height of the crisis from 6 January 1993 until the end of August that same year. The conditions imposed by the Serbian authorities on the handover of the airport to UN control, included ensuring that the airport was used exclusively for the transportation of humanitarian aid for the civilians trapped inside the city. Only UN personnel, peacekeeping delegations and certain accredited members of the world press would be allowed to fly in or out.

The grounds of the airport had to be secured in such a way that no one could cross in or out of the city. Like all missions, advanced planning takes time and I was tasked with the job of obtaining up-to-date maps and photographs of the region. I also had to find information on the logistical strengths of the belligerents.

SARAJEVO AND THE BALKANS

Accurate information was scarce to say the least, but I was able to present a document covering everything from the estimated number of people being held within Sarajevo, to their ethnic breakdown. Not everyone was a Muslim – there were still a considerable number of the Christian and Jewish communities who had been unable to leave before the blockade was set up by the Serbs. After that it was too late and there was no way they could get through the front lines of the two sides.

I had the additional advantage of being able to draw on the knowledge of our Yugoslavian legionnaires who knew first hand some of the problems we were likely to face. This was another clear example of the unique strengths that came from the multi-national, multi-racial composition of the Legion. This local knowledge and the language skills would help us to gain the confidence of both sides. There is no doubt that this played a major part in the eventual success of our mission.

One person in particular played a major part in this and put himself at great personal risk on several occasions. Just how important a part he played will be made clearer as the story unfolds. A lesser man would have stayed quietly in the background. By the time we were ready to leave I felt that I already knew a lot about the country. We were told that the airport was fairly modern having been built to cater for the 1984 Winter Olympics.

Photographs showed Sarajevo as a modern city with skyscrapers, parks and a river running through it. The Adriatic coast had long become a favourite with British holidaymakers and the yachting fraternity. The mission was going to be a doddle – after all, I had just come back from a so-called war. Boy, was I wrong! What awaited us was a nightmare world, far worse than anything I could have imagined.

On 6 January, the advance party consisting of the command staff, of which I was part, and a combat company, flew out from Corsica on a civilian Air France 747 to Zagreb, the Croatian capital, after which all traces of normality disappeared. I thought that I had seen the worst of mankind while serving as a police officer, but again I was in for a big surprise.

It was almost midday when we landed at Zagreb and for security reasons we manhandled all of our freight off the 747 and onto a UN-chartered Soviet Ilyushin II 76 transport aircraft for the short hop to Sarajevo. We knew that this would be a new experience when we were issued with flak jackets and told to sit on them rather than put them on. This was not because the seating was uncomfortable, but because the combatants on the ground from both sides used the approaching aircraft for small-arms practice. This was borne out by the number of pieces of 'gaffer tape' stuck on the outside of the aircraft over the bullet holes as a kind of instant repair. A bit of a wake-up call for us all and you could see the sudden realization that this was going to be dangerous on the faces of every one of us.

We took off our green berets and replaced them with blue United Nations ones. We were now officially part of the United Nation Protection Force, or UNPROFOR as it was better known. This was the first 'peacekeeping' mission to be undertaken by the Regiment and our operational methods would have to be adapted to comply with the UN rules of engagement. It would be a test for all of us, regardless of rank.

The flight itself was uneventful but I noticed that we had climbed well above the normal altitude for what was a short-haul flight. We were obviously flying well above any anti-aircraft batteries which might be tracking our flight from the ground. Fifteen minutes out from Sarajevo we were instructed to put on our helmets and, once we were on the ground, to wear our flak jackets. We were also told that as soon as the ramp went down we should not hang about on the tarmac admiring the view, but get into the protection of the earth banks as quickly as we could.

Suddenly the nose of the aircraft was pointed towards the ground as we made our approach. We literally screeched to a halt, were off the runway and into the parking zone within two minutes of touching down. They had done this sort of thing before. When the rear ramp of the aircraft was lowered we saw a corridor made up of armoured airport fire engines between ourselves and the huge banks of earth which protected the terminal. We had only taken a few steps when there was the sound of gunfire and of bullets impacting against the sides of the fire engines. Seconds later, one of the lads who was only a few paces ahead of me fell to the ground holding his left leg. He had been shot in the calf by a round which had been deliberately bounced under the fire engines. The marksman couldn't see his victim, but the chances of hitting someone were fairly high. The two lads nearest to him dropped what they were carrying and grabbed the victim as we all ran for cover.

Word had obviously got out to the belligerents that a changeover was taking place and this was their way of welcoming us. Fortunately the injury was only a flesh wound, but it made us take seriously the security warnings given to us by the unit we were to replace. They were a French Regular Army unit who had been in Sarajevo for the past four months and had suffered quite a few casualties, including three dead. It was the first time that any of us had heard about this and it came as a bit of a shock.

Geographically, Sarajevo is the easiest of cities to put under siege. It is situated in a valley with towering hills on all sides giving a clear field of fire into all areas of the city. The entire city was within easy range of the tanks and heavy mortars of the Serbian Army. Snipers controlled most of the road intersections, making it impossible to move about the city on foot or in non-armoured vehicles. Every exit from the city was closed off by Serbian forces. All aid coming in by road was channelled onto one road from the north which was controlled by the Serbs.

The two opposing factions were only yards apart in some places and were engaged in World War One trench warfare tactics. This was our introduction to Sarajevo. I had gone from looking forward to the deployment to being very, very apprehensive about the whole affair. I spent my first night sharing accommodation in an unprotected two-storey office block in what had been the cargo area of the airport, with the guys I was replacing. They filled me in on their last four months of hell and it was obvious that they couldn't wait to get on that plane. There were no shelters of any kind and if the building had taken a direct hit that would have been the end of us all. I didn't sleep a wink because of the regular detonations of exploding shells. To me they sounded yards away but I was assured that although close, they were outside the airport perimeter.

Our first task was to find safe accommodation for the rest of the Regiment who were due to join us the following week. I was appalled at the conditions these men had been living in. They had done nothing to improve their conditions or take even the most basic security steps, like putting sandbags on the flat roof of our building, or protecting the windows from direct fire or shrapnel from exploding shells.

What the hell had they been doing? I wasn't surprised that they had suffered so many injuries. That would all change, but we could do little before the others arrived. It was decided that we would install two of the companies on the ground floor of the main terminal. The airport was closed to civilian traffic so that wasn't a problem. Indoor recreation facilities would have to be created as it was impossible to go outside.

General morale and fitness would play an important part in the months to come. The admin company, medical facilities, catering and the two other combat companies would take up residence in the customs warehouses, and the command section would sleep and work from the customs office block where I had spent my first night. Major changes would have to be made to increase security, with the construction of proper guard posts and shelters round the perimeter, and the main buildings would be properly protected by blast banks, with all windows covered over. That was the plan anyway, but it would take some time to implement. In the meantime we just had to make do with what we had. Some of the offices exposed to direct fire were closed off immediately and we started to mark out the zones to be occupied by the incoming companies.

Under the airport occupation agreement both sides had designated 'observers' who seemed to be able to walk about the airport with little or no restriction. But that all changed immediately. They weren't pleased in the least and complained loudly, but from the day we arrived we issued new passes that limited their access to areas where they could check humanitarian goods coming through the airport, and that was it.

They were denied access to all buildings, including our eating facilities. All civilian catering staff were dismissed which just left two girls, one Serb and one Bosnian, who worked for us officially as interpreters. They lived in our block but even they had their freedom to roam severely curtailed. They had both worked as UN interpreters before the troubles had started and had

UN security clearance. Even so, we were careful about what documents they saw.

The customs compound comprised a detached two-storey office block, a single-storey warehouse and a two-storey warehouse. The office block was turned into our headquarters, with the offices on the first floor and the living accommodation on the ground floor. There was also a large air-conditioned Portakabin at the end of the office block protected by an earth bank.

The larger of the two hangars was made up of two two-storey buildings with a covered hall giving access to the two wings. The ground floor of one wing was turned into a hospital which would be manned by the medical staff from our own regiment. The ground floor of the other wing was turned into accommodation for the admin company and one of the combat companies. The upper floor was divided into a conference hall and a sports area where we could play badminton and volleyball. The floor above the hospital became an equipment store.

An observation post was built on the flat roof of the central hall which gave us a good view towards the city. The conference hall would be the location for future peace negotiations between the two sides. Space was at a premium for everyone, with the HQ block having to accommodate ten officers, five NCOs and ten other ranks, plus the two female interpreters. There were also a toilet block with showers, a Dutch signals detachment of six men, our offices and operations room. It was a bit of a squeeze to say the least, but these were not normal times. For power we had a generator accessed by scrambling through a window in the shower room, which was always interesting if you happened to be having a shower at the time.

The terminal building also had to accommodate all the other personnel required to operate the airport: firemen, air traffic controllers, aircraft handling staff, mechanics and engineers, all of whom were crucial in keeping the airport operational. The military airlift ran seven days a week. All the staff were from the UN and most were delighted when they saw the changes we were about to make to their living conditions. We had to strike a happy balance with those already there, assuring them that any changes we made would take into account their requirements. Overall morale improved for everyone and as the risk factor was reduced, life would become a lot easier.

As already described, our first night at the airport was a real example of what was to come. If the intention of the opposing sides was to make an impression on us, they certainly succeeded. Some of the heavy artillery and mortar rounds were landing just yards from the perimeter fence but we would have to wait until morning to find out if there had been any damage.

There was a dusk to dawn curfew imposed on us by our Colonel with only essential personnel venturing out to perform specific duties. To us, the uninitiated, it sounded as if the rounds were landing on our heads. The ground shook continuously and it took a considerable effort to force yourself to lay your head on the pillow and shut your eyes. I have no doubt that a direct hit would have come right through the building.

We were told that the key word in UN peacekeeping was 'transparency'. Everything we did was meant to be open to scrutiny. That little bit of brilliant thinking had been put in place by politicians who never had to put their own lives on the line, and of course it didn't apply to them. Perhaps it wasn't explained properly to us but our Colonel took the words 'everything we did' to mean just that. It didn't say we had to let anyone see how we went about achieving what we did.

Although I was still under the orders of my own Colonel in Chief and the head of the BOI, I was also working with a captain from a French specialist Intelligence regiment who had been assigned to the Regiment for the duration of our mission. We got on very well and he treated me as an equal as far as work was concerned. I respected his rank and we had a good working relationship. I will just call him Captain D. There were times when it was difficult for him to integrate with the Legion officers – he was there to perform a particular task but there were those who wanted him to perform normal regimental duties.

My first task was to build up a portfolio on the military liaison officers from the Bosnian and Serbian armies. The information we had was very sketchy and nobody had prepared such a dossier for our arrival. In fact, I was beginning to wonder what the departing regiment had been doing over the last four months. The girls were able to provide me with some details and I set out to photograph secretly the delegations from both sides when they were invited to our base to be introduced to our Colonel. I also photographed the inspection teams who came to the airport each day. It was a bit of basic police work and I set up a collation system for the incoming intelligence, no matter how unimportant it seemed at the time.

I had been allocated one of the new French four-man, light-armoured, combat vehicles known as a VBL. It was fabulous and could take small-arms fire without any problem. The shape of it was designed to deflect the blast from a mine or small rocket, although it wouldn't withstand a direct hit from an anti-tank rocket or anything like that. It was certainly a hell of a lot better than the Land Rovers the British Army use in Afghanistan today.

I was listed on the UN personnel declaration as a 'staff driver', and was issued with a UN driving licence and ID pass which gave me right of access to all territories in the execution of my UN duties. In principle this gave me a certain freedom to roam in areas that perhaps I should not have been in. It was common practice for the Serbs to look into vehicles but they did not have the right to search them.

Under the UN rules we were not permitted to use any equipment which could be interpreted as being used for spying. This included photographic equipment, but I fitted video recording equipment into the VBL which I could operate remotely using a tiny fibre-optic lens. I filmed wherever I went as I wanted as much footage as possible inside the Serbian military base at Lukavica Barracks, the Serbian Army HQ just to the west of the airport. The layout of the camp was of interest and I wanted to see what kind of equipment was lying about in the form of tanks and heavy artillery. Most of it was hidden under camouflage netting and invisible from the air. I also wanted to see who was coming and going at the base and was able to match some of the faces with those of the 'neutral inspectors' at the airport. They were obviously there to pass on information about us and it was good to know who was who.

Captain D and I visited the Serbian base frequently and I would drop him off for his meetings, then drive further into the base to turn round. I would venture further into the camp on each visit until one day I was stopped and turned back by a rather irate Serbian officer. I was in the middle of a huge parking area which was filled with row after row of old soviet T62 and T76 main battle tanks, which quite frankly looked the worse for wear. What had attracted my attention was a row of vehicles with covers over their loads. From the outline I took it that they were missiles of some sort, and quite large ones at that, but I was ordered out of the area and would have to try at a later date to get a better look.

The American pilots bringing in supplies had reported that they had been 'lit' by tracking systems when they had flown over the area, but these looked much bigger than I would have expected if they were anti-aircraft missiles. Back at the airport I reviewed each day's filming with Captain D and would copy anything out of the ordinary to be sent back to France for further analysis. We both thought that the covered loads needed further investigation. Perhaps an expert would be able to tell us what they were from their outlines.

Each night was a repeat of the first and the shelling got more intense with the arrival of the rest of the Regiment. This had been going on for over a year and the civilian population must have been totally traumatized. I had only been here for a fortnight and it already seemed like months. We were taking casualties from sniper fire and although the injuries were not serious it was only a question of time before there would be a serious incident. Our transmission aerials and satellite dishes were on the roof of our building and had to be repaired every night. One particular sniper seemed to be using them for target practice during the day if he had nothing else to shoot at.

It was getting colder every day and I was glad that we had been issued with proper cold-weather gear back in Calvi. I am not ashamed to confess that I had brought out several pairs of ladies' tights with me. They were far lighter and just as warm as the thick arctic underwear that some of the lads had bought in specialist survival shops at specialist prices. I was not the only one and we had the last laugh when the others were literally 'freezing their balls off'. After a couple of weeks at -20°C those without girlfriends were begging us to get tights for them.

TRAINING TO BE SHEEPDOGS ON 'THE CROSSING'

Every night, hundreds of Bosnians would try to cross the airfield to freedom. It was our duty to stop them, round them up and take them back to the outer fence where we released them back into the city. It was all part of the UN agreement to keep the airport open for humanitarian aid flights.

Dobrinja was a Bosnian enclave on the city side of the airport linked to the heart of the city by a series of deep trenches. The objective of those trying to cross was to make it to the village of Butmir, and from there over Mont Igman, before making the long trek to the coast and freedom. Ammunition was brought into the city by the same route and we also knew that Islamic militants were getting into the city via this route. This was long before the Bosnians dug the famous tunnel to freedom under the airport. Even that was not used by everyone as it was controlled by criminal gangs who demanded large sums of money from those trying to flee the city, so even after it was built the nightly crossings continued.

Each night as darkness fell, up to eight VABs (armoured personnel carriers), with a full combat group in each, went out onto the crossing zone. They would then spend the entire night during the hours of darkness rounding up those trying to cross. Night vision equipment had to be worn as any light from our vehicles helped the Serbian snipers and machine gunners to lay down a carpet of fire. Working in groups of three or four VABs, they would form a protective shield round those trying to cross. The majority of those trying to cross were not combatants but women and children who were desperate enough to try and get out of the city, away from the living hell that was their daily lives.

The VABs would surround a group to protect them from the gunfire and a VAB would be driven into the protected area, with the rear of the vehicle facing away from the direction of the gunfire. The legionnaires then had to get out onto the open ground and direct the civilians into the back of the

VAB. This was extremely dangerous work being done under a constant hail of fire. There were many stories about how the Legion was helping the Serbs by lighting up the 'crossing zone' with searchlights, but there was absolutely no truth in this. The legionnaires suffered casualties and risked their lives every night to try and protect these desperate people. This went on all night, every night. If those rounded up were uninjured, they were taken back to the hole they had cut in the fence and barbed wire. It was a policy that none of us were happy with but these were our orders in keeping with the UN agreement for control of the airport.

Many of the civilians were seriously injured or killed and had to be taken into our medical facilities at the airport where the Legion doctors and medics worked hard to save their lives. Some lived, some didn't. The only good thing to come out of the situation was the wealth of expertise our medical staff were gaining and each night they were more capable of treating the victims more successfully.

I cannot emphasize enough the outstanding bravery shown by the legionnaires who had to go out there night after night to help others. Not surprisingly I take exception to journalists like Jeremy Bowen of the BBC, who alleges in his book *War Stories* that the legionnaires 'played games' with the Bosnians trying to cross. When we first heard these stories being bandied about by the press, I was sent to the Holiday Inn in Sarajevo where Jeremy Bowen and his fellow press colleagues were staying, to invite them to go out on the crossing at night to experience for themselves what was happening. Not one of them took up the offer. Perhaps the bar was a more attractive option. My humble contribution to this nightly exercise was to take my turn to go out onto the crossing in a VBL, along with the duty officer for the night, whose job it was to orchestrate the use of the VABs. I would be driving with the use of night-vision goggles and the sky would be full of tracer rounds. You have to have total confidence in the armour of the vehicle and, in particular, in the bullet-proof glass of the windscreen.

My first night on the crossing scared the shit out of me and I didn't even have to get out of the vehicle. Watching the tracer rounds arc almost in slow motion across the tarmac just feet off the ground, is impressive to say the least. The sound of the impacts on the side of my VBL made me jump and it was impossible not to duck on seeing a tracer round heading for your windscreen. There were five of us sharing this duty and we decided to do three nights in a row which gave us twelve days off crossing duties. We would come in at about 6.00 am and were allowed to sleep until midday. It was also the quietest time of the day as both sides seemed to be in bed as well.

MY FIRST CLOSE ENCOUNTER

On the afternoon of 19 January 1993, just weeks after we had arrived, I was sent out to take a look at a Serbian area at the western end of the runway. There had been reports of heavy machine-gun fire from the area, aimed across the runway at the village of Butmir. One problem was that the rounds were passing just behind our sentry post at the northern entry to the airport. Anyone going to or from the post was getting caught up in the crossfire.

I went out in my VBL to the area in question but was unable to see anything because of the earth bank. The only answer was to get out, climb to the top of the bank, peek over the top and have a look. It might sound crazy but I was wearing the distinctive blue helmet of the UN and was wearing my flak jacket. I didn't exactly stand up on the top of the banking and wave my hands about, but lay down as I approached the top and then scanned the area with my latest gadget, range-finding binoculars. You focus on an object, press a button and the distance and compass bearing to it come up in your vision. The buildings were a bit shot up and obviously uninhabited. They were little more than a pile of rubble. At first glance the area was deserted but as I looked a bit closer at the detail, I could see trenches running between the buildings. It takes time to realize what you are looking at, especially if it is the first time you have been so close to buildings adapted for urban warfare. All our training had been done in whole buildings, not ruins, which would actually have been a lot more realistic.

Objects began to take form and I could see that there were anti-personnel mines all over the place in the long grass in front of the buildings. I had just taken a photograph when all hell broke loose. There was a machine-gun post at the centre of the buildings which opened up on me. I didn't know if he was aiming low intentionally, but I was struck in the face by bits of rock-hard earth kicked up from the bank. My camera was knocked clean out of my hands and I slid down the side of the earth bank. I lay there for a while to regain some of my composure before scrambling back to the safety of my VBL. I sat there for five minutes and was about to drive off when I realized that the camera was still lying at the foot of the earth bank. I quickly retrieved it before heading back to my office rather quicker than I had left it. Unknown to me, the guard post at the entrance gate had witnessed the incident and had reported it to the operations room. Once I was back inside the safety of the office I realized that I was sweating despite it being below zero outside, and I was shaking. I was still wearing my helmet when the Colonel came into the room, asked me if I was all right and pointed at my head. I took off my helmet and was surprised to see a large tear in the cover and a 4-inch groove in the helmet just right of centre. These were still our own metal helmets, but not long after the incident we were issued with new Kevlar helmets which were reported to be capable of stopping a bullet from a pistol at 5 metres.

The groove must have been caused by a bullet but fortunately only my pride was hurt. It gave me one hell of a fright and I wouldn't be doing that again in a hurry. The camera was all right with just a few scratches on the body. When I eventually got the film developed and blew up the images, I was able to identify the exact spot where the machine gun was located. We protested to our Serbian liaison officer and to his credit that particular firing position was removed. He had been told in no uncertain terms that if he hadn't done it, we would. I think they were starting to recognize that they would have to work with us and that we would not be intimidated.

Like everyone else I had to take my turn on night guard duty. We were so short of personnel on the ground that even the Caporal Chefs had to do guard and take their turn as checkpoint controller at the UN roadblock on the only road into the city from the airport. This particular checkpoint consisted of a large container filled with sandbags which blocked half the road. A VAB was positioned sideways across the remaining gap and only pulled back behind the container to open the gap to let UN vehicles and escorted aid convoys in or out of the city. It was only manned during daylight hours and after the checkpoint was withdrawn for the night, all hell broke loose along that stretch of road. The trenches were so close that they could lob grenades at each other.

Despite all this, my workload was no heavier than anyone else's. We were all working seven days a week and stress levels were high. It was just as well we had built adequate recreational and sports areas at both the terminal and the freight complex. They were well used by everyone and the two-level running circuit inside the main terminal was particularly popular.

The buildings round the airport had been shelled extensively. Everywhere you looked was destroyed and yet there were people living in these bombed-out ruins. One of the strangest sights was the lines of carpets strung out between the buildings. I didn't understand why at first until it was explained to me that the hanging carpets blocked out the view between the buildings and afforded a limited protection to anyone walking in the streets behind this screen. The carpets also had a dampening effect on any bullets fired through them, reducing the severity of any injury – simple but very effective.

Because of the ruined state of the buildings, it was very difficult to locate the snipers who could be hiding under a dislodged slate or in the depths of a darkened room. There was not a single piece of glass left in any building on the perimeter of any enclave. I decided to devise a simplified way for our men on guard or observation duties to identify the location of the snipers. When you looked at any of the buildings, there was so much optical clutter that describing where the shot had come from was impossible. I could see only one solution so I set about photographing the view from every observation post in a series of close-up linked images. Eventually I had a complete 360-degree coverage of everything facing the airport. I sent the films back to Calvi for development and had A4 size prints made of each shot. When the photographs came back, I joined them up to give me the overall view from each OP. This was still a confusing mess so I covered them with acetate and hand drew the outline of each building. I then included in the drawing any feature of interest or points specified by the observers. This enabled me to provide a simplified image and gave each point of interest a reference number. I supplied a copy of the view to the relevant OP and kept one for the operations room.

When a sniper fired, all the observer had to do was call in the reference. For example: 'Post 3, B6'. We then knew instantly the location of the sniper and it was easier for the observer to add a reference if a new location was spotted. The system was an instant success and we were able to establish a series of favorite locations used by the snipers thereby enabling our commanding officer to formulate a response to the problem. It was a lot of work but the end result was well worth the effort. The system has now been adopted by the French Army as a whole, as standard procedure when in a combat zone anywhere in the world. Using computers and digital technology has made the task a lot easier, but the principle is the same. I am proud that I have been able to contribute in a small way to a system that can save lives.

UN headquarters in Sarajevo were in what had been the Post Office and Telecommunications (PTT) building. It was located on the dual carriageway that led into Sarajevo about halfway between the airport and the city centre. This building, which comprised ten floors and an additional two below ground level, was of fairly modern construction. Up until then it had not been a target for direct shelling, although some shells and mortar bombs had landed very close to the compound. All UN activity in the city was coordinated from the building and it was not in the interest of either side to put it under direct attack. All countries taking part in the UN operation had a senior military presence there and as a result it was difficult to maintain operational security. There were some countries that were openly biased towards the Serbs.

There will always be those who will seek to profit from any situation. The UN Security Council agreement states that all principal equipment used in a conflict zone must be the property of the UN. The only exception to this rule are armaments defined as personal weapons, such as assault rifles. The agreement also states that only equipment which can be described as defensive may be brought into a combat zone. Armoured personnel carriers are defensive but a tank is offensive. All countries brought in their own vehicles but to comply with the regulations they were then bought by the UN.

This made it easier to rotate units with heavier equipment already in place. Every vehicle to be used was brought into a large parking area and valued by a UN purchasing officer, who authorized payment in full to the country owning the vehicle. Up to this point, not a problem. As can be imagined, this involved hundreds of vehicles being lined up, inspectors walking down the line counting the number, and that was about it – it was a numbers game without each vehicle being individually inspected. One eastern bloc country in particular would tow in old BTR personnel carriers which wouldn't even have an engine and pass them off as operational. Perhaps there was a backhander, but certainly no one batted an eye and they had to know it was going on. The vehicles would then be towed away never to be seen again – or at least not with the same identification numbers. For all I know the same hulks made several visits to the assessors. We were told that it was none of our business and not to rock the boat. I was to witness other financial scams later in the tour.

One problem we were facing was the extremely cold weather. This was to be expected in a region that had hosted the Winter Olympics, but living in the Mediterranean, and having spent so much time in the heat of Africa, meant that we were more used to adapting to the tropics than the cold.

A deep snow covering in an urban war zone is not good news. Every night anti-tank and anti-personnel mines were scattered by both sides on the approach roads and surrounding areas. This meant that all access roads to the airport had to be cleared every day before we could start normal operations. That on its own was bad enough, but when the surface was covered in 2 feet of snow it was very bad news indeed.

There were two principal entry points to the airport and two emergency ones. The main entrance faced the city and was in no-man's land, as was the main road, in fact the only road, into Sarajevo. At least during daylight hours it was controlled by ourselves and on the whole relatively safe if you obeyed the rules. The northern entrance was a different kettle of fish. It ran between two of the most contested areas and the battle lines were within spitting distance of each other. We had to use this road to gain access to the Serbian area of Lukavica where their military barracks were. We knew exactly where the principal combat posts were on either side of the road; we also knew where the Serbian tanks were inside of the ruined buildings. It was always a relief each time you crossed the area without incident. All hell could break loose at any time and it was just too bad if you were caught in the middle. This area had seen so much fighting that there wasn't a house left intact or a tree that had not been sculptured by the thousands of rounds fired by both sides. These were not the images you saw on TV or in your morning paper. This was the reality of war on the front line, not a piece done to camera in a safe zone with images and sounds dubbed into the background. Each time I drove along this road I got a shiver down my spine and sometimes I had to make the journey two or three times day. Even today, when I look at photographs I took of this area, I get a strange feeling.

Once a week we brought the two sides together for peace negotiations at our compound within the customs area at the airport. Neither side trusted the other and we had to bring them to the meetings simultaneously in our VABs. Both sides insisted on having a dozen armed soldiers with them, but once they were inside our compound they had to hand over their weapons. Each was taken into the building separately, searched and disarmed before being taken into the conference room. If it hadn't been such a serious affair it would have been comical.

Each soldier was given a cloakroom ticket with a number in exchange for his weapons. Everything had to be written down in a book and signed in against the number on the ticket, for example: 'Ticket No. 8. AK47 assault rifle with 200 rounds, 6 hand grenades, a 9mm automatic pistol and two ammunition clips (full) for said weapon, a combat knife and bayonet'. There were no exceptions and the generals had to submit to the same body search as their bodyguards. At first they objected but they soon got used to it. At the end of the meeting they handed in their cloakroom ticket and got their weapons back, signed out and were driven back to the safety of their own areas at exactly the same time. Timing was vitally important for the security of all concerned. Had one group reached safety before the other, there was always the danger that there would be an attempt to take out the other. These were high-ranking people and their deaths might have been worth the resulting scandal.

There was no doubt that they hated each other and their problems were not going to be solved over a cup of tea.

During these exchanges we were able to gather valuable intelligence while escorting the delegates. As I explained the Legion is a multi-lingual body like no other, and we made sure that the legionnaires acting as escorts spoke or at least understood the local language. They were on strict instructions not to speak a word but to listen and report everything that was said. Some of the revelations were startling. They discussed everything from what they wanted from the negotiations, to what they were seeing and noting – our defences and equipment, and how they would go about attacking us if it came to the crunch. As a direct result we always made sure that nothing vital to our security could be seen during their visits and from then on the small side windows of the VABs had their flaps closed, blocking their view.

These meetings were the first time any sort of dialogue had been started between the warring parties. It was early days but at least it was a start. The first couple of meetings were short-lived affairs with the participants exchanging verbal insults at the tops of their voices and could easily have turned into a brawl.

As usual I set about photographing the faces of everyone to add to our files – you never knew what might be of use at a later date. For example, when we compared the earlier photographs with those taken at later meetings we noticed that some of the more senior figures had been present in the background in the guise of bodyguards.

Yugoslavia is a major crossroads between the racial and religious cultures of Western and Eastern Europe, and the Middle East. For centuries one party or another has tried to dominate the region, but since the death of Tito things have gone from bad to worse. He may have ruled with the iron fist of a dictator, but at least the region found a certain stability. Now that he was gone the country had fallen apart. There might have a fragile peace at the time but it was only a question of time before the violence came to the surface again. We were always being reminded that we were there to make peace not war, and that we should be transparent in everything we did. The only military actions we undertook had to be for our own protection and not deemed to be aggressive, or show any bias to any one side in the conflict. That is a lot easier said than done. To the outside world it appeared a clear-cut case of victim and aggressor, but in this case the victims were far from innocent.

THE REALITIES OF ETHNIC HATRED

The bottom line was that the Serbs and Croats were both engaged in the process of ethnic cleansing. They both believed that their homelands had been stolen from them by systematic colonization over the centuries. In particular the Serbs also reckoned that they had been pushed out of their homes in towns and villages by an invasion of Muslim communities from the Middle East.

There is no doubt that there was some truth in this, but it did not justify the blatant torture and killings which we were now seeing before our own eyes. Everything that was happening there had a lot in common with what was going on between the Israelis and Palestinians today. At the end of the day both sides have to share the blame and come to some kind of agreement. There can be no outright winner in either conflict, but sadly it will never happen.

The final straw for the Serbs of the old Yugoslavia was no doubt the declaration of the independent state of Bosnia and Herzegovina on 29 February 1992. The siege of Sarajevo followed immediately, resulting in the war I was now in the middle of. The Serbs cleared entire villages of their Muslim populations and if they did not want to occupy the vacated homes, they burnt them down or destroyed them with artillery or tank fire. Young men were executed in front of their parents, wives and children, then the women were raped before being driven into the hills along with the aged and infirm.

As winter continued, it was easy to see why Sarajevo had been chosen to host the 1984 Winter Olympics – the snow-covered mountains touched the very edge of the city. The different venues were within a 15-mile radius of the city centre which made it a perfect location.

The Olympic village was of typical 1970/1980s eastern bloc construction, comprising four-storey concrete blocks of flats close to the airport, in the district of Dobrinja. The new flats were called 'Airport Settlement' and still had the Olympic rings painted on the front of them, overlooking the airport. The rings were now used by the Serbs for a different kind of sport – target practice for their tanks, with a case of beer or a bottle of the local booze the prize for a direct hit.

A big problem for the occupants of the city was the lack of electricity and heating. When the newer parts of the city had been built, an underground heating system had been installed in the state-owned tower blocks. The heating and electricity came from a coal-fired power station and was one of the first things to be destroyed by the Serbs at the beginning of the conflict. All alternative fuel supplies to the city were cut off by the Serbian blockade. The result of this was that anything that could be burned was either cut down or broken up to be used in the improvised cooking stoves which were also the only source of heat in the freezing conditions. There was not a tree, hedge or wooden fence post left and expeditions into the heavily mined wooded areas around the city often resulted in grievous wounds or loss of life.

Only the minimum basic food supply convoys were making it into the city. Although these supplies were supposedly for distribution to everyone, in reality it was far from the case. The Serbs delayed every aid convoy for days on end, except those that were clearly marked as coming from Christian charities destined for distribution by the Christian community within the city. This meant that some supplies were getting through while others were held up or simply stolen.

We were not meant to be involved in the humanitarian aid distribution process, but it was obvious that things were not as they should be. Parts of the city were under the protection of the Ukrainian UN force who were openly biased towards Serbian nationals isolated in the city. Something would have to be done.

Our first ploy was to make the international press aware of the problem but again they were only interested in news that was visual, with lots of explosions close to the reporter who was supposedly risking his life to bring you the latest earth-shattering news as it was happening. I have come to the conclusion that politicians only want the public to hear things that make them sound wonderful, and journalists only want the public to hear how good they are at telling you all about it. What the news actually is doesn't matter. We even had instances of Ukrainian armoured cars coming into the airport for fuel, filling up, driving out of the airport, going round the block and offloading the fuel into Serbian tanks before coming back in for a second top-up. Again, no one wanted to know because it would cause a diplomatic row.

There was not a bit of ground within the city limits that was not planted with vegetables – even the grass borders at the sides of the roads were used to grow potatoes. You could tell where the snipers had a clear line of fire into the city – these were the only places where the grass grew as no one would take the risk of venturing there during daylight hours. There were parts of the city which could not be shielded from sniper fire and we watched the different reactions of people when they moved into the more exposed areas. Some would run straight across without any hesitation, others would stand for a while before they built up enough courage to go, while others just froze on the spot for hours, unable to cross. The latter often waited until an armoured car came along. It would then slow to a walking pace allowing dozens of pedestrians to cross the gap using the vehicle for protection. The snipers always opened fire, trying to shoot under the bodywork in the hope of hitting someone, reminding me of our experience when we first arrived. There were even those who seemed to have given up, in a way. If they got shot, so be it. They might have lost a loved one and felt that they had nothing to live for. They would just walk across the gap at normal walking pace while the bullets flew round them. I was convinced that the snipers were playing games with these poor souls, for surely they couldn't miss. They would let some of them get across safely, whilst others would be brought down seconds before they stepped into cover. If we were passing we would brake and try to protect them, but they never even looked at us – they just didn't care. I had never seen that before and found it very sad.

The siege was having another strange effect on the women of Sarajevo.

In an attempt to maintain family morale, they made considerable efforts with their personal appearance. Hair stylists were kept busy, they took great care with their make-up and dressed smartly. It was their way of showing defiance. The death rate in the city was so high that the football stadium had to be used as a graveyard, but despite all of this there was an air of determination about the population. Everything was in ruins. There was no public transport, the tram system had long since ground to a halt and any private cars left running had been commandeered by the Bosnian militia. They cut sheet-metal plates and fixed them to the sides in an attempt to protect them. All glass was removed but there was so little fuel available that the only way to move about the city was on foot.

By now I had compiled an extensive dossier about both sides. Apart from the intelligence I gathered myself while driving Captain D about, both the Brits and the Americans provided me with whatever I requested with no questions asked. The Americans had a Hercules which was fitted with a camera pod. It was based in Ancona in Italy and flew in to Sarajevo on a regular basis. The pilot must have been one of the worst in the Air Force because he kept overshooting the runway, forcing him to fly low over the Serbian barracks and most of the city as he circled back to make another approach. On the next visit he would bring me copies of the photographs he had taken during his aborted landings. These helped me build up a picture of the trenches and, more importantly, gave me the chance to see certain areas and objects from different angles. For example, a tank position might be totally hidden from the front but exposed from the rear. He also had a thermal-image camera which would show men and equipment hidden in the trees above the city.

The Serbs in particular protested about these fly-pasts and threatened to shoot down the aircraft. They even gave away anti-aircraft positions by locking on to him with acquisition radar. When this happened the aircraft would fire off their anti-missile defence systems, called chaff. It was always spectacular as the decoys flared out behind the aircraft, rather like an upside-down firework display.

Quite a few of the aircraft were hit by small-arms fire as they approached or took off from the airport. Some of the crews had armour installed in the cockpit for protection. Fortunately there were no disasters in my time but I do know that one of the Russian aircraft suffered major damage a few years later and can still be seen lying on the grass at the western end of the runway. I must pay a tribute to the Russian crews – they were the only ones who continued to fly when everyone else had suspended operations because it was too dangerous.

The British Forces HQ was in the small town of Kiseljac, which is about 30 miles north of Sarajevo. This was in territory controlled by the Croatians and was deemed not to be a combat zone. The unit was based in a hotel with all the normal amenities one associates with hotels: rooms with baths, a proper restaurant, a bar and a nightclub. They even had an outdoor tennis court and there was a riverside path they used for jogging when they felt like it.

I am not bitching or saying that they had it easy. It was just that the contrast from the hell-hole we were living in made it hard to accept that we were only 30 miles down the road. It was like being in another world. In fact, it was another world. To get there we had to pass through two Serbian, one Bosnian and then finally a Croatian checkpoint. At the latter two you only had to slow down to let them open the barrier, but at the main Serbian checkpoint it was a completely different situation. As this was the only supply route into the city, every single aid convoy was checked again and again, lorry by lorry, box by box. They would insist on counting every round carried by each member of the UN peacekeepers, then note the number against each name, then double check it again against the manifest supplied by the UN. It could take hours and in some cases days for a convoy to pass.

Captain D and I had to go to Kiseljac almost every week and were always escorted by a unit from the CRAP. The first couple of times we suffered the same delaying tactics as everyone else, but this is not how the Legion works and it was time for a change. Normally there was a young teenage girl armed with an AK47 manning the barrier. This was a psychological game the Serbs were playing to show that even a teenage Serb could bring the UN to a halt. No one had seen fit to dispute the point but that was about to change. The convoy drivers didn't care – they could only do one mission at a time and if they spent it sitting at a roadblock they didn't care.

On our third visit to the checkpoint we encountered the tail of the queue about half a mile from the barrier, but Captain D told me to overtake the waiting vehicles. The usual girl left the lorry she was checking and came over to us, shouting and waving her rifle about. Captain D got out of our VBL and in quiet, broken English, told her that if she didn't open the barrier there and then, the only bullets she would be counting would be coming out of the end of his rifle. The guys from the CRAP were out on the road and I heard the sound of their weapons being armed. It was no contest. There were only four of them at the checkpoint and ten of us looking as if we meant every word. The girl almost fainted and went as white as a sheet. She started to speak then thought better of it and turned to walk to the barrier. Captain D caught her arm and told her quietly but firmly that in future when we turned up at the crossing he expected the barrier to be opened with the minimum of delay. She was asked if she understood. She nodded and walked over and raised the barrier. She even half saluted as we drove through.

From that day on, whenever we appeared, the barrier was opened with the minimum of fuss and we were waved through. We always slowed down, smiled at her and gave her a wave. On one occasion I had to stop beside her as we waited for the road to clear. She was a pretty girl and had a nice smile. As I pulled up I opened the door, said hello and smiled back at her. In heavily accented English she said, 'Are you French legionnaires?' I told her we were and that was the end of the conversation as she briskly walked off to speak to one of her colleagues. I had no idea what she said but it looked like 'I told you so.'

We had called their bluff and it was another minor victory which would enhance the reputation of the Regiment. Word of what had happened seemed to spread quickly amongst the Serbs and everyone noticed a change for the better at all the Serbian checkpoints. They were more civil and the delays got much shorter, at least where the Legion was concerned. Since our arrival in Sarajevo we had been obliged to wear our flak jackets and helmets every time we went outside. We therefore felt very strange and vulnerable when we got to Kiseljac and were told to leave our flak jackets and helmets in our vehicles. It was a welcome return to normality, but you could sense that everyone was hesitant to relax just in case it wasn't true. It was only then that we all realized just how stressed we had become.

The British Military Intelligence unit worked in the hotel and Captain D and I had obtained clearance to make full use of their facilities. The Major in charge was very helpful and, in particular, I was able to use their 3D computer mapping system. It was a system which let me visualize any given location from another in three dimensions. For example, I could put in the coordinates of any known Serbian tank position in the hills overlooking Sarajevo and the computer showed me the view the tank crew had of the city in 3D. I won't go into all of the possibilities that this system presented, but needless to say I used it a lot. I can't thank the Major enough for his help – he never once objected to my requests.

We also enjoyed the luxury of eating in the hotel restaurant. There was even a menu with a choice of starters, fish or meat as the main course, and not only were there desserts but a cheese board. Coffee was taken through to the lounge. We had to get back through the checkpoints and into the airport before dark, which was a shame because dinner was served in the evenings from 8.00 pm and included a wine list. You have no idea what psychological effect all of this had and how we dreaded the hour when we knew that we had to put on our flak jackets for the drive back to hell. Although no one said anything you could see it on the faces of my colleagues as we left the security of Kiseljac behind. I was convinced that the UN personnel working outside Sarajevo did not appreciate just how bad conditions were for the civilians and military living inside the boundaries of the city that were under siege.

One unusual supplement to our diet came in the form of Marks & Spencer Christmas puddings. The Brits had been sent so many as gifts from the UK over the festive period that they were sick of them. I was more than happy to ease their problem and loaded several boxes into the back of my VBL. They went down a treat with the lads back in Sarajevo, so much so that I was asked to try and get some more on my next visit. I was even able to find some custard powder to go with them. It was a small thing, but when you have been forced to eat nothing but ration packs for weeks because the Serbs had been delaying our supplies of fresh food, any little treat was gratefully received.

This reminds me of another comment by Jeremy Bowen in his book. He says that he bought bottles of Bordeaux at the back door of the Holiday Inn from legionnaires who, he claimed, were each getting a bottle supplied every two days and were then selling them on at £30 a bottle. To put the record straight, our six months in Sarajevo were totally alcohol free – not even a beer. If you think about it, there were 600 of us and if what he said was correct, that would mean we were receiving over 9,000 bottles a month. That's a lot of transport space when we couldn't even get basic food in. The Serbs would never have let all that wine through their roadblocks anyway. To our minds this was another example of 'If it sounds good – print it journalism'. It doesn't give you a lot of faith in the quality or reality of anything else being reported.

I have referred to the main road into Sarajevo being manned by a UN checkpoint during daylight hours. It was not uncommon for either side to open fire suddenly on each other using mortars, rockets and heavy machine guns. It was up to the person in charge of the UN checkpoint to decide when it became too dangerous to sit out there exposed to any stray rounds, and to make a tactical withdrawal to a more sheltered spot a hundred yards up the road.

I was duty controller one day when a couple of mortars exploded 20 to 30 feet away, showering the VAB with debris and shrapnel. Sometimes it was safer to sit it out and pull back into the semi-shelter of the armoured vehicle. You were then stuck inside the VAB for the duration of the shift and all personal needs had to be taken care of in it. You couldn't even open the door to get some fresh air. Thank God they were fitted for chemical warfare and had a system for filtering and recycling the air.

After passing through this checkpoint on your way into the city, the road went under a flyover where the Bosnians had set up a heavily manned checkpoint of their own. They never stopped UN vehicles or an escorted convoy, but they had a fear that the Serbs might suddenly rush down the road and would be able to drive into the centre of the city before anyone realized what was happening. Once onto the dual carriageway there were three main buildings of strategic importance. The first was a ten-storey building which used to be the offices of the daily newspaper. It had been heavily shelled but they continued to print a broadsheet from the basement deep amongst the debris as a symbol of defiance. It had been the first building to be destroyed in 1992 when the siege began.

The next building was the UN Headquarters which has already been described and along the roadside were several high-rise housing estates which had been built in the late 1970s as the city expanded on the lead up to the Winter Olympics. They had been austere, clinical places before the war, but now they were half burned-out ruins where people lived a miserable existence under a constant fear from snipers and shelling. At first glance the buildings looked abandoned, but they were actually full of life. However, no one walked the streets, there were no children playing in the open spaces and there was nothing to indicate that whole communities were eking out an existence here. All the sounds you associate with a lively city were missing: traffic, people talking on street corners, the sound of feet on pavements … nothing – and yet an entire city was living within the confines of these buildings.

It was a different thing when you walked through the sandbagged entrance to one of the blocks. Suddenly you were surrounded by noisy children playing within the relative protection of the stairwell. Women chatted loudly at doorways. It was like something out of a science fiction film where humanity had moved below ground to avoid the aliens. Suddenly someone would dash from behind a building heading for the cover of the next, quickly followed by the crack of a sniper rifle. Sometimes they made it, sometimes they didn't.

I didn't live through the horrors of the London, Coventry or Clydebank blitz during the Second World War, but this had to be as bad, if not worse. At the end of February, I was driving on my own into the city centre down snipers' alley to pick up Captain D from a meeting. I had just passed the Holiday Inn where all the armoured TV Land Rovers were parked. If the press had known just how 'unarmoured' their vehicles really were they would never have gone out in them again.

Suddenly a smartly dressed woman made a dash across the junction. This was a particularly wide and dangerous crossing which was clearly visible from the Serbian sniper positions overlooking the town. She wasn't even halfway across when she seemed to be picked up by an invisible hand and was thrown backwards onto the road. I braked automatically and came to a halt alongside her, keeping my vehicle between her body and the sniper. Without giving it a second thought I got out of my VBL to go to her assistance. As I rounded the front of my vehicle I was aware that something had just passed close to my head. It was immediately followed by the sound of the bullet impacting on the bonnet of the VBL – then I heard the shot. It was like rewinding a film. There was a second impact and my reflexes made me look behind me. The window of my door had starred due to the impact of the second shot, but hadn't broken. I remember thinking 'Shit I'll have to replace that.'

I turned my attention to the woman who was lying at my feet, crouched down behind the VBL for protection and felt for a pulse. She was barely alive. The bullet had entered just below her right collar bone. I was surprised at how little blood there was at the point of entry and couldn't see an exit wound. I applied a field dressing to the wound and did the best I could for her under the circumstances. Her only chance of survival was if I could get her to the UN hospital in the basement of the PTT building.

This meant I would have to radio for assistance, but as I half stood to open the door, another shot rang out followed by a second about five seconds later. The sniper was obviously using a bolt-action rifle. Fortunately two VABs were making their way back to the airport and pulled up to give me assistance. One of them was fitted with a 20mm heavy gun which could be fired from inside the vehicle. When another shot from the sniper rang out, the VAB opened up with a long burst of deadly accurate fire into the sniper's location. I don't know if he was hit or not but no more shots came from that particular position. Within seconds we had the woman inside one of the VABs and lost no time in getting her to the hospital, but she was dead before we got her into theatre. Closer examination of her body showed that the single shot had deflected off the collar bone, severing her spine before exiting from the small of her back. She was better off dead and just became another statistic of the conflict. There were so many similar incidents every day that there was a strong chance that her body was never reclaimed by her family.

This was only one of the tragic deaths I would witness over the coming months. Although you don't think about it having an effect on you, it obviously does. Some cope better with this kind of stress than others. You build up a kind of immunity to it over the years and I had had a head start on many of my younger colleagues having had my share of dramatic situations and dead bodies during my time as a police officer. I can understand why so many ex-soldiers suffer from post traumatic stress. Being confronted with this sort of thing without warning can cause many people to suffer problems at a later date.

It has been interesting to hear doctors and surgeons in the UK, who have suddenly had to deal with the dying and injured out on the streets of London, after the Underground bombings, speaking about the horror and stress they were feeling. Normally they only have to deal with the victims after they have been removed from the carnage surrounding the incident. It is normal that the people in the front line, the Police and emergency services, will experience conditions that anyone would find stressful. The military in war zones have to deal with the same kind of problems, but have the additional problem of performing effectively while under fire. I am no expert in psychiatry but I can see that we are going to have a huge problem caring for the members of our armed services coming back from present-day conflicts. Some of these problems are due to the fact that they are not fighting in a classical war, army against army. We are asking them to be peacekeepers, instructors, builders and suppliers of humanitarian aid.

At the same time we expect them to fight terrorists without the backing of the local civilian population. In fact, they don't even get much support from the civilian population in their home countries. Is it any surprise that they come back from a tour of overseas duty confused and troubled by their experiences? There are few organizations at home willing to put the money and effort into helping them. Those who do work on a voluntary basis get very little help from the government. If politicians saw some personal gain from publicly backing such organizations, they would be right in there smiling at the cameras at every opportunity, and no doubt the money would be flowing.

As far as our own casualties went, we had been lucky up to this point, although one young English Legionnaire had managed to get himself shot in the hand, and then in the shoulder, on two separate occasions. He was treated in our own hospital at the airport and made a full recovery, staying on in Sarajevo until the end of the mission. He was one of the legionnaires that Jeremy Bowen said was playing with those trying to cross the airport at night. His commanding officer refused to let him go back out on the crossing and assigned him to duties that kept him indoors well out of harm's way. Everyone felt that the old adage about third time lucky should not be put to the test.

We were now getting a clear picture of where the snipers were located. There had been a steady increase in the number of incidents reported of personnel working at the airport coming under fire and being injured. Our Colonel in Chief decided that enough was enough and issued orders which allowed us to take appropriate action to stop the attacks. This was a brave decision on his behalf as it was in direct contravention of UN standing orders. The UN 'Rules of Engagement' dictated that only weapons classified as defensive could be brought into 'peacekeeping' zones.

A rifle known as 'The Big Mac' is made in the US. As can be imagined it has nothing to do with eating a hamburger. It is the Tac50, 12.7mm sniper rifle manufactured by the US armaments company McMillan and there is nothing about it that can be described as defensive. This rifle is aggressive in every way, from its range and power to the ammunition it fires.

The problems we faced in Sarajevo prompted us to use a weapon that had the capacity to out-range the snipers, who up until now were operating with impunity. We had tested this particular rifle back at our base in Calvi and had a couple of them in the armoury back there. Two of the lads from the CRAP went back to Calvi to pick them up and brought them into Sarajevo in guitar cases. What kind of music they made was open to interpretation. The object of the exercise was to reduce the danger to our men from snipers by eliminating, or greatly reducing, their numbers. It was also important that no one knew what was happening or where the return fire was coming from.

Special concealed areas were prepared in the terminal building, on a need-to-know basis. These posts were manned during daylight hours by the snipers from 4th Company and members of the CRAP. The weapons were fitted with lazer sights capable of working with pinpoint accuracy at long range. The rifles had an effective range of well over a mile and required forward spotters to identify and mark the exact location of the sniper with hand-held lazers. It was a bit like the technique we had used in Iraq when guiding missiles on to the target. Our sniper picked up the spot from the hand lazer and simply overlayed his lazer sight onto the target. He might not have been able to see the actual sniper from his location, but such was the power of this weapon that it had the capacity to penetrate a brick wall at these extended ranges. The results were spectacular and the enemy snipers had no idea what had hit them. None of them would survive to tell the tale and it took less than a week for the message to get through. There was a sudden lack of volunteers to take up sniping positions anywhere near the airport.

Our weapons were returned to Calvi as soon as we were satisfied that all sniping against our personnel at the airport had stopped. Sometimes extreme problems require extreme solutions. The 'rules of engagement' have since been changed to allow for circumstances such as this and there is no doubt that our Colonel made the correct decision at the time.

It was hard for us to sit back and not intervene when we saw blatant aggression from one side or another. We had the military capacity to stop attacks from either side, but our hands were tied by UN red tape. It must also be said that the competence of some UN military commanders left a lot to be desired. They were not prepared to take any decisions that might have an effect on their careers at a later date, and who can blame them when the political negotiators seemed to be on an ego trip. Most of the UN political mediators were well aware of the intense media coverage they could generate as soon as they set foot on the tarmac at Sarajevo airport. They were often more concerned about how they looked on camera, or came over on TV, than they were with actually solving the problems.

One particular 'chief negotiator' always made sure that the press were aware of his arrival in Sarajevo for 'secret' talks. He would fly in wearing a helmet and full body armour, which was the right thing to do. As soon as he was inside the security of the terminal but out of sight of the awaiting press, the body armour would come off and he would change into a suit and a tie. Fine, but those with him had to keep theirs on, giving the impression that he was the only one brave enough not to be wearing any protective clothing.

To the viewers, here was this brave, super-cool man, but we were instructed to form a physical screen around him, but never within shot of the press cameras. There was always a VAB right beside him with its rear doors open should anyone as much as sneeze in his presence.

We had been having problems obtaining fresh supplies of food for ourselves. As a result, we had been eating combat rations for weeks. This very same VIP arrived from the UK at lunchtime and demanded a hot meal before chairing the negotiations. Our Colonel in Chief informed him of our situation and offered him a gas stove and a ration pack. He was so infuriated that he got back on his private jet and flew back to the UK. The negotiations had to be cancelled. You would have thought that he was a 'Lord' or something!

He was not the only politician to behave this way. The majority seemed to have no moral fibre and were only out to advance their careers. A blind eye would be turned to the truth if it did not suit their own goals, regardless of the suffering caused by their inaction. The whole conflict was one big deadly game, being played out by everyone concerned. Both sides went to extreme lengths to hide their military capacities from the United Nations observers.

On one occasion, satellite and aerial photographs arrived on my desk showing the location of tanks and mortars which were in place in contravention of the negotiated agreements. We headed out immediately to the location with a UN inspector, only to be delayed for hours at a checkpoint. When we eventually got to the location in question there would be nothing to be seen. On another occasion I received photographs of a mortar battery being set up in a grassed area in the middle of the Bosnian town of Butmir, just outside the airport boundary. Our inspection team was delayed as usual but when we got there we received an overtly warm welcome from the locals, who asked us to stay and take part in the school fête which was in full swing. From the fresh tyre marks in the grass we could see that the photographs had not lied. I showed them to some of the town's leaders hoping that it might put them off repeating the exercise. They just looked at them with blank faces and shrugged their shoulders. I have no doubt that the mortar unit was back in place ten minutes after we left.

As part of field tests, we were supplied with a high-powered electronic imaging system. I installed it in our observation post on the flat roof that joined the customs warehouses. It could be linked to a digital camera or a computer and let me photograph and download images of objects in great detail, at a distance of up to 10 miles. I hate to think about how much it was worth. I could even photograph the faces of the tank crews high in the hills, and in such detail that you could identify the individuals. The system could also be used at night allowing us to monitor troop movements after dark. When this information was collated with conventional intelligence we were able to draw up a fairly accurate map giving detailed locations and strengths of the opposing forces in and around the city.

The aerial photographs drew our attention to one particular trench that ran up to an old farm building just outside the fence close to Butmir. There seemed to be an abnormally high volume of movement to and from this particular ruined building and it was not in an area close to any Serbian or Bosnian front lines. We had heard that the Bosnians had, or were, building a tunnel under the airport from Butmir to Dobrinja, but this was the first real indication that it might be true. It was in an area we had no real access to and so it was impossible to verify what was going on.

The existence of the tunnel did not pose a problem to us, but it would have to pass directly under the runway, with the risk that it could collapse under the weight of the huge transport aircraft using it. If this happened, a vital humanitarian link into the city would be lost. A substantial part of the aid was flown in by air and could never be replaced by road transport. The Bosnians naturally denied the existence of the tunnel but they still refused to let us approach the building in question. We emphasized that our concern was structural safety and would say things to them like, 'Hypothetically speaking, if such a project did exist, you could do this or that to reinforce certain parts where there might be a weight problem.'

There was no doubt that the Serbs also thought that the project existed and constantly shelled the rather exposed building, posing another problem. The building was less than a hundred yards from the runway and we noticed that the trench was particularly busy when an aircraft was landing or taking off because the Serbs would stop shelling to let the aircraft land. It eventually got to a point where not only did the Serbs continue the normal barrage, but they would open up with everything they had. This put the aircraft at such risk that the pilots refused to fly and the airlift came to a halt. The only planes that continued to fly were the Russians as they needed the money.

One Serbian tank position was less than 500 yards from the building in question and the rounds they fired would be at such a low trajectory that they would ricochet off the ground without exploding if they missed the target. The shells would scream across the runway before impacting on the earth banks protecting our base near the customs area. We never did resolve this matter satisfactorily but the Serbs agreed that the tank posing the greatest threat would hold fire while there were aircraft movements. It did mean that there was a huge chunk of the airport that became no-man's land because of the risk of accidentally driving into the path of a tank shell.

It was important that we continued to build a relationship with both sides outside the official meetings. To this end we visited the residential areas as often as possible, until our visits became part of their daily routine. We even got on first-name terms with some of the locals and the kids would swarm round us if we had chocolates or sweets.

The children were always a great source of information and the sweets more than paid for themselves. We were aware, of course, that the children were also being used to get information from us. Every little boy wants to sit in a fire engine and it is the same with military vehicles. You couldn't afford to forget that the radio equipment had nice illuminated frequency readouts. The children were told to memorize them and report back to Dad, so that they could monitor our frequencies. I always covered the dials with electrical tape before we went on these missions. For security reasons the frequencies were changed every day, but despite this I would see bits of paper, with the day's frequency written down, taped to the dashboard.

We had a direct landline laid into the headquarters of both sides in case of emergencies. Captain D had managed to develop such a good working relationship with a Serbian officer that he would call us on the landline to tell us that point X was about to be shelled and that we had five minutes to move out anyone we had in the area before the bombardment started. If we had passed this information on to the Bosnians, he would have simply stopped calling us, putting the lives of our men at risk. Sometimes it would prove embarrassing when we suddenly left an area and it was attacked minutes later. But it was all part of the game. On one occasion the message was relayed to me from our command post and, as I left, the first mortar bomb exploded exactly where I had been parked less than thirty seconds earlier. It wasn't long before the locals realized what was going on and headed for the shelters as soon as we started to pull out, so in a way we were able to save their lives without actually telling them. I often wondered if this was why we were told in the first place – perhaps they weren't all bad.

Another Close Encounter

On 25 March 1993, I had my second and closest encounter with death. Our headquarters were still located in the offices of the customs area at the time. The administration office was on the first floor of the building and although the windows could only be seen from the last building in a row of small cottages in the Serbian area of Kasindolska, we normally did not use that particular office after dark. We knew that the cottage was used as an observation post directing fire onto the village of Butmir on the other side of the runway.

The windows were taped and covered in paper to block the view, but after dark, if there was a light on in the office anyone moving about would be silhouetted in the window. The windows weren't sandbagged but it was a fairly safe location. We didn't wear any of our body armour inside the building as it was fairly cumbersome and we didn't think we needed it.

Darkness fell at about 4.30 and I had not quite finished with a report. Without thinking someone walked into the office and switched on the light. My American friend Joe was working at the computer and I was bent over behind him reading the screen when a single shot came through the window. The gap between our heads was only a matter of inches and we both felt the heat from the bullet as it passed between us before imbedding itself in the office wall. We were both showered with the glass from the window giving us both multiple superficial cuts to the side of our faces. By pure reflex we threw ourselves onto the floor landing in a heap, with Joe's chair on top of us.

After we had assured each other that neither of us was badly hurt, I reached up and turned off the light. There were no other shots. We edged forward and tentatively looked out of the shattered window towards the cottage. In the semi dark I could make out two figures standing out in the open next to the corner of the building. They were looking back at us through binoculars and laughing. One of them made a gesture with his middle finger before taking a slug from a bottle and walked back into the house. When we turned round there was a whole group of figures in the corridor outside the office. We confirmed that we were OK but had to go to our camp hospital to have our cuts cleaned and some small pieces of glass removed. Nothing vital had been touched which was lucky as some of the glass had scratched my glasses.

An incident like this affects you more than you think or are prepared to admit at the time. It is the suddenness of it that gets to you. In combat you expect to get shot at, but the first time I was shot at, followed by the woman being hit at the junction – then this – does have an effect on you.

A couple of days after the incident I had a chance to recount what had happened to the Serbian liaison officer. He said nothing at the time, simply raising his eyebrows. He asked me to point out the building where the shot had come from and half an hour after he left the cottage received a direct hit from a tank round. A coincidence? Who knows. At our next meeting he smiled and said, 'No more problems, I trust.' We never mentioned the subject again and I got the impression that a broken fence had just been repaired. It's a strange world we live in.

Both sides were aware that we had no authority to step in to enforce a ceasefire. As a result we were forced to play the roll of spectator to some of the more flagrant acts of aggression. One afternoon I was driving our Colonel in Chief back to the airport from a meeting at the PTT building. As we approached the entrance to the airport, a movement caught my eye in my wing mirror. The old Olympic village (Bosnian) and the Serb district of Kasindolska were, in times of peace, joined up by the road we turned off to get into the airport. A Serbian T72 tank had pulled out into the road behind me and was using our VBL as cover to get nearer his intended target. Seconds before I turned into the airport the tank opened fire, the round passing only feet over the top of our heads. The ground shook and there was a clap of thunder as the round screamed overhead to explode in the building directly in front of us. I put my foot to the floor, shot past the open barrier and the guard room and in behind an earth bank. The tank came to a halt opposite the gate then opened fire again, before reversing back up the road. Its heavy machine gun was pouring a constant stream of lead into the buildings as it went, preventing anyone from even thinking about firing back. Minutes later it was back from whence it had come. Not a shot had been fired in return. Everyone had been caught on the hop, including ourselves.

The damage to the targeted building was extensive and a cloud of dust hung over it. As it cleared we could see people scrambling out of the debris. Later we learned that twelve people had died in the attack. Our Colonel made a formal complaint about the incident and thankfully it was never repeated. We had no authority to open fire on the tank as we were not being targeted directly. We had the ability to destroy the tank and one of our Milan missile units had it in its sights throughout the incident. It was another example of the political restrictions the UN enforced on us.

The Serbs also had an old Russian four-barrelled 40mm anti-aircraft gun which they kept in a garden shed just across the road from the entrance to the airport. The Bosnians could not see where it was kept, but every night after the road into the city was closed, the Serbs would pull it out of the shed into the garden and open fire with it onto the high-rise flats less than half a mile away. This would continue for fifteen minutes before it was pushed back into the shed for the night. The gun's crew would then go home for their tea and probably watch TV. Again we were powerless to do anything about it and could only sit and watch the firework display, knowing that people were being killed at the receiving end. It was a crazy situation.

As described earlier, aid convoys were subjected to long delays at the Serbian checkpoints. Despite the humiliation being experienced daily by UN personnel, during my entire stay in Sarajevo, I never saw or heard of any senior UN official turning up at any of the checkpoints to complain. When the aid convoys eventually reached the outskirts of the city, they had to report to the airport to get permission from both sides to drive down the last stretch of road past our checkpoint and on into the city. Many of the convoys were from charities that had collected aid in their home countries for the people of Sarajevo. Although well meaning, the convoys posed a particular security problem for the civilians who accompanied them. These convoys consisted of lorries from all over Europe, including the UK. Most were ill equipped for the extreme winter conditions and the drivers and their helpers had no idea how to conduct themselves in a war zone. Until this final stretch into Sarajevo, they had been able to drive at night, but once here it was strictly forbidden.

One convoy from Scotland arrived at the last Serbian control point just before darkness fell. The Serbs did not want them on their patch overnight so pushed them through with instructions to drive straight to the airport. On leaving the Serb checkpoint at Kasindolska they had to turn right for the short 200-yard run into the safety of the airport where they would park overnight before being escorted into the city first thing in the morning. The UN checkpoint had been withdrawn for the night and, as usual, all hell was let loose between the opposing factions. The person at the head of the convoy thought that it was a waste of time going to the airport as he could see from his road map that it was only 5 miles to the city centre. When he came to the junction where he should have turned right to get to the airport, he turned the convoy left heading for the city along the stretch of road controlled by our checkpoint during daylight hours. They hadn't gone 200 yards before they were fired on, both sides thinking that the other was making an unauthorized dash into the city. The Bosnians thought that it was a Serb attack and the Serbs thought that the Bosnians were trying to move military supplies from one area to another.

The convoy came to a sudden halt in the middle of the road nose to tail when the lead vehicle was hit. The fire was then concentrated on the last vehicle which was also incapacitated, making retreat impossible. We saw and heard the firing from the airport and knew immediately what had happened because of the non-arrival of the convoy at the airport. We therefore got on the hotline to both sides and managed to get an agreement for a ceasefire, but it took time. In the meantime the convoy was taking a pounding.

Some of our VABs had been fitted out with lights to illuminate our UN symbols and flags, to enable us to make emergency runs into the city from the airport. It was rare that this happened and only when we had a medical emergency which required us to get to the main hospital in the PTT building. Once the ceasefire was in place, and with the agreement of both sides, our VABs were sent out to recover the occupants of the convoy. No one had any idea what we would find, but fortunately the occupants of the lorries had reacted quickly and most had made it into the ditches at the side of the road. Sadly one woman from Edinburgh had got out of her lorry and tried to run back up the road, only to be cut down by both sides. She died instantly. There were a couple of other minor injuries, but considering the weight of fire that had been directed at them it was a miracle that there had been only one fatality. The legionnaires rounded up the survivors and recovered the body before heading back to the airport for the night. The lorries had to stay where they were for the time being and would be taken back to the airport at first light.

Once inside the security of the airport the survivors started to realize how lucky and stupid they had been. The incident was 100 per cent their own fault and for once neither the Bosnians nor Serbs were to blame. Rule number one: when in a war zone, do as you're told. The lorries were recovered in the morning, but as we expected, half of them had been relieved of their contents during the night. They were so shot up that they had to be towed back to the airport and most of them ended up as scrap.

The Serbs were furious that their orders had been disobeyed and as a result closed their checkpoint to all non-military convoys for two weeks. Fortunately for the occupants of the city, most of the essential aid such as food and medicines were brought in by air. As it turned out, like most charity convoys, this one was carrying clothes that were not suitable for, and articles that were not essential to, the survival of Sarajevo's residents. It was all very well intentioned but tee shirts and summer dresses were not what was needed there, it had been a waste of time and effort, and had sadly cost a life. This was not the only incident of its kind – others resulted in a much greater loss of life.

From contacts with families at home, we were aware that events in Sarajevo were receiving extensive coverage on French television, much more so than was being reported back in the UK. Because of this our Colonel in Chief was concerned that our families and friends back in Calvi would be worried about our safety. News of injuries could not be kept secret and we knew that rumours would be rife. To combat this he decided that a weekly news video should be recorded and sent back to Calvi for showing in the camp cinema. Families and friends would be invited to attend the screening and everyone, we hoped, would be a lot happier.

We tried to present a calm relaxed image of our lives in Sarajevo, showing footage of the men using the sports facilities we had constructed. It was important not to film anyone in the background wearing body armour and everyone in camera wore a beret rather than a helmet. The videos included shots of convoy escort duties passing through beautiful countryside and I made sure that there were no scenes of burnt-out houses or dead animals lying in fields. It could have been a film for the Sarajevo tourist board. Messages were recorded for their children by happy, smiling fathers. When I look back at these videos you could be forgiven for thinking that our mission was one big holiday and would never have known that we were in a living hell.

There was one amusing incident when a senior officer was making an introductory piece to camera while standing on the steps at the entrance to the PTT building. He was not wearing any of the offending clothing and was in the middle of telling everyone how peaceful it was, when an artillery shell screamed overhead and exploded about 50 yards away showering us in debris. I don't know which one of us hit the deck first, but when I looked up, the officer had disappeared inside the building. Needless to say that particular footage did not make it back to Calvi. Which side had sent us the present was not clear but we had obviously been observed filming and whoever it was had decided to make their own contribution to the video. It struck me later that we were guilty of manipulating our own families through the power of the camera, in exactly the same way the press were manipulating the public – what you see on TV often has nothing to do with the truth.

Three hospitals were operating in Sarajevo: the civilian one in the city, the UN one in the PTT building and our own one at the airport. Several legionnaires had suffered minor gunshot wounds while working on airport crossing patrols and our medical staff were fully occupied every night striving to save the lives of the injured civilians the patrols were bringing in. We had an operating theatre installed in the customs warehouse and the doctors were forced to operate under less than perfect conditions. They had no choice but to perform complicated surgical procedures on cases which really required specialist surgeons and equipment. Literally hundreds of civilians had their lives saved by our doctors and Legion medics, who worked non-stop through the night, every night.

The walking wounded were taken back to their own side of the fence after treatment, but it was not unusual to be dealing with the same person shot for a second or third time, days later, such was their desperation to leave the city, and who could blame them. For every one 'crosser' that we turned back, twenty made it. Despite knowing that we had to perform this duty, we felt that we were putting our own lives at risk every night for something that was ineffective, and that we did not want to do. But these were our orders from the UN.

Each morning the more seriously injured were either transferred to the civilian hospital or to the UN one in the PTT building. Most ended up with the UN, simply because the civilian hospital could not cope with the demand on their services.

We were more interested in what was being brought into the city and confiscated large quantities of military hardware and ammunition. Every morning we would search the crossing area and would recover the objects that had been abandoned during the night. When they saw that they were about to be caught, the culprits would dump their weapons, hoping that someone else would pick them up and take them into the city. There was everything from assault rifles and ammunition to hand grenades, communication systems and maps showing the latest Serbian positions, to RPG7 anti-tank rockets.

One chap we arrested was a Turk who had deserted from the REP eighteen months earlier. He had not known that it was his old regiment, never mind his old company, that was controlling the airport that night, so he got quite a shock when he was brought before his former company commander. He had served for quite a few years, had been a junior NCO in 4th Company and had considerable experience in the handling of mines and explosives. He was detained and flown out in the morning to the American base in Ancona in Italy. I never did find out what happened to him after that.

CHAPTER 15

Our Darkest Hour

We had two VABs fitted out as ambulances, clearly marked as such, with large red crosses on every side. They also carried two big flags with red crosses and the UN symbols. On 11 February, one of our regular patrols was visiting the Bosnian village of Butmir when they were asked for urgent medical assistance. A woman in the village was about to give birth, there appeared to be complications and she required immediate hospital attention.

The nearest facilities were our own hospital at the airport, but under the agreement we required permission from the Serbian authorities to bring someone into the city. She would have to be transferred to Sarajevo after she had received emergency treatment. Permission was obtained and one of our ambulances was sent to Butmir to pick her up. There was an emergency entrance we could use for missions of this kind, saving a long detour through the roadblocks to get to the airport, and there was provision for exactly this kind of emergency within the airport operational agreement.

Our medical staff were standing by to receive her and within minutes of her arrival within our compound, she was whisked into theatre. I had opened a window in our command room to film the arrival of the ambulance and was intending to go across to the hospital to film our doctors helping the woman give birth. It would be nice to show that there were positive things going on in the middle of all the mayhem. The birth of a baby was always good news.

The driver of the ambulance had just parked his vehicle and was climbing out of the driver's door when the VAB took a direct hit from a mortar. Three more heavy mortar rounds exploded beside the vehicle, one on the Portakabin at the end of our block and a fifth one hit the entrance to one of our observation posts within the compound. Legionnaire 1er Class Benco and the co-driver of the ambulance were seriously injured. The driver had several shrapnel wounds but none serious. Fortunately the others were still inside their VABs and, although concussed, were otherwise uninjured. The Legionnaire inside the observation post was protected by the sandbags but suffered ear damage from the shockwave. The attack had taken place within seconds of the woman being taken inside the building and there is no doubt that it was directed by someone inside or with a view into our compound.

I realized afterwards that I had heard the first round coming over the roof of our building, seconds before the explosion. The injured were rushed into the hospital to be treated beside the woman they had just gone out to save. She gave birth to a healthy child but sadly Legionnaire 1er Class Benco died from his injuries. Our doctors meanwhile worked hard to save the life of the ambulance co-driver, Legionnaire Novokouski. It was obvious that he needed major surgery beyond their capabilities and a special flight was laid on to take him to Paris for treatment. His life was saved, but sadly he lost his leg.

The investigation showed that the mortar rounds were fired by a Bosnian mortar battery situated not 50 yards from the home of the woman who gave birth. Despite our protests, the Bosnian authorities never accepted any responsibility for the outrage, nor expressed any sympathy for the loss of life and injuries caused. Instead, they issued a statement saying that this was another example of Serbian aggression.

This was not the only time that the Bosnians had been prepared to commit atrocities on their own people in an attempt to gain the sympathy and attention of the world press. There was the well-reported incident when the market in the centre of Sarajevo was hit by mortar fire. The market was controlled by Bosnian Mafia organizations and criminal gangs with influential connections with local politicians. The market was in full swing and was a hive of activity when several mortar rounds exploded in the square. The carnage was horrendous. When you are dead, you are dead, but the injuries caused by mortar shrapnel can be appalling. The high-explosive content is designed to fragment the metal casing into twisted chunks of red-hot metal which are thrown outwards and upwards at 30° from the point of impact. The aim of this kind of attack is to kill and maim as many people as possible. Very little structural damage is caused to property.

This incident happened at a time when things had been relatively quiet and Sarajevo was not making front-page news. There was immediate worldwide condemnation of the Serbs for the atrocity and the UN did very little to counter these claims. The twist in the tail was that because of the height of the buildings surrounding the square, it was impossible to fire mortar rounds into that location from Serbian positions. The angles of impact indicated that the mortars had all been fired on a short high trajectory and had come from an area of the city held by the Bosnians. The UN team of experts called in to examine the location submitted their report which stated clearly that the mortars could not have been fired from a Serbian position. They had no proof of who had been responsible but if it wasn't the Serbs, and it certainly wasn't us, then it must have been the Bosnians themselves.

Again, Jeremy Bowen says in his book that he heard rumours from the French that the Bosnians were responsible, but that he personally didn't see any evidence of it. Even someone who was not an expert in this type of investigation and who had visited the market would have seen that it was impossible for the Serbs to have made the attack. The allegations weren't pressed by the politicians at the time because it was felt that it was not in the public interest to do so as it would only make peace negotiations harder.

This kind of incident makes it very hard to do your job objectively. The Serbs were the public bad boys – and they were. There is no doubt that they were engaged in war crimes including ethnic cleansing, but that does not mean you have to turn a blind eye to incidents like the mortaring of the market. It is another example of where human life means nothing compared to the cause. If a few people go to meet their God, so what – after all, it is an honour for them to have died for their cause. It's just that no one told them that.

On one of my visits to the UK base at Kisiljac, I met a Korean technician who was servicing a rather large, top-of-the-range, photocopier. I commented on how a machine like that would make my life so much easier as I only had a small black and white portable one back in Sarajevo. 'Not a problem,' he said. 'Just get yourself down to Zagreb and you can take your pick from the UN warehouse.'

When I got back to Sarajevo I immediately arranged to fly to Zagreb the following day. At the UN procurement department I was shown to a large warehouse with office equipment of every kind stacked to the roof – a veritable Aladdin's cave. I had been asked to try and get a photocopier for our administration office as well as for myself. A civilian clerk asked me what I required, filled out a couple of forms, stamped them and gave me a guided tour of the facility. There were desks, office chairs, computers, filing cabinets and hundreds of photocopiers. I could have equipped the entire Regiment from what was stacked in that warehouse.

The clerk explained that it was all bought and paid for by the UN. There was easily over £500,000 worth of equipment in that warehouse alone, and I could see that there were several identical warehouses within the complex, but I have no idea what was in them. He said that everything that had not been distributed by the end of the mission in the Balkans would be written off and would disappear into the black market. He was quite open about it and didn't see what was wrong with the system. Another scandal that no one spoke about.

Transport was provided to take me back to the airport and I set off back to Sarajevo with two colour photocopiers that could print double sided, sort documents in page order, and automatically bind and staple them into the finished article. At no time was I asked to sign for anything and had only shown my UN ID card to the clerk when I first arrived. Back in Sarajevo I explained how the system worked. Within a couple of weeks each of our companies had made the trip to Zagreb and re-equipped their offices.

If this is how the UN runs every mission it undertakes, then there are a lot of people making an awful lot of money supplying goods that nobody really wants or needs. There didn't seem to be an effective audit system in place and there must have been other things that the money could have been spent on, like refugee relief, for example. Both sides had been in the habit of manipulating and intimidating UN personnel at every turn. It took exceptional patience, firmness and the ability to stay calm in the face of extreme provocation. On the whole we were lucky to have officers and senior NCOs of the highest calibre who were prepared to take decisions which put the safety of their own men above all other considerations.

From the moment we arrived it was made clear to us by UN politicians that we were expected to carry out the mission without prejudice. There were even those who thought that we should let every aspect of our operations be open to inspection by both sides, including our command and control set-up, communications, everything. They lived on another planet and I am glad to say that our commanders thought otherwise. Our Colonel in Chief was a man of large stature and had the personality to go with it. The Serbs in particular are a tall race, but our Colonel was able to face up to them eyeball to eyeball. Our highest-ranking NCO was a Croat by birth, and when we first arrived he had a few problems establishing working relations with the belligerents, in particular the Bosnians. In the end he got through to them and played an important part in establishing a certain level of trust, while maintaining a healthy respect for the Regiment's military prowess. Both men made it clear that they would not stand for any acts of aggression against us. Unfortunately it didn't stop the attack that killed Legionnaire Benco. Even the changes we had made to our living conditions, and our professional approach to security, did not go unnoticed by observers working at the airport. I am sure that the message that things had changed was passed on up the line to their bosses.

Daylight hours on the whole were safe enough, but as soon as darkness fell both sides behaved like animals. Once we had dealt with the snipers around the airport, the main danger was sniping and shelling within the city itself. When a bullet or shell misses its target it can travel a long way before it hits something, and that could be you or the building you were in. It might not be deliberate, but that makes no difference when it hits you and a careless moment could cost you your life. Whenever we left a building, even within the compound, we put on our flak jacket and helmet. Even crossing the 25 yards from the office block to the canteen was dangerous. No one loitered outside, not even for a quick fag. Not many legionnaires smoke but those who did had a great incentive to give it up. It gives a whole new meaning to the expression 'I'm dying for a fag'.

A Change of Tactics

At the beginning of March we knew that there had been a change in the Serbian strategy when the outfield of the airport started to get a pounding from artillery and mortar fire during daylight hours. The intensity and range increased every day until the shells were landing just outside the earth banks which protected the buildings. The danger was that it was inevitable that stray rounds would start to fall inside our compound and onto the terminal buildings. It became so intense that all normal activities came to a halt and because of the danger to aircraft landing or being offloaded, the airlift was suspended. Even the Russians stopped flying. At the worst of this period over 2,000 rounds fell within the airport perimeter every day. Miraculously not one legionnaire was injured as a result of the shelling, but everyone's nerves were jangling. I now know what it must have been like for the soldiers in the trenches during the First World War, and we were in relative safety. The constant noise and shaking of the earth was what got to you. It just didn't let up, day or night.

External movements had to be kept to a minimum, but our duties had to be performed as usual. We did notice that if we drove towards an area that was being shelled, it came to a halt and would resume once we had passed. Once we realized this we were able to make our way to and from different parts of the airport as we wished, but the situation could not be allowed to continue.

Again our Colonel showed what he was made of and gave the order for our heavy 120mm mortars to be brought over from Calvi. On their arrival they were set up and aimed at the Serbian base at Lukavika. He let it be known that if one more Serbian round fell within the confines of the airport, the Serbian HQ would be reduced to rubble. We were on very good terms with the US Air Force based at Ancona and they agreed to make some dummy attacks on the Serbian barracks using F16 fighters. Because of our reputation, our threat was taken seriously and the shelling stopped well before the deadline. Over 50,000 rounds had fallen in close proximity to our positions in just under three weeks. The silence that followed was almost as nerve-racking as the bombardment. There was still the nightly shelling of the city, but its intensity was nothing compared to what we had just been through. All the same, every time a shell exploded, even in the distance, we jumped.

Sarajevo's power station and fresh water supplies had been destroyed by the Serbs at the very beginning of the siege. The nearest working power station was 50 miles away in a Bosnian-controlled area but the power cables had been brought down where they crossed areas held by the Serbs. We managed to get an agreement to let us run a temporary landline into the city which could carry enough power for the hospital and essential services during daylight hours. The Serbs were able to cut it off as darkness fell but would suddenly restore the power in the middle of the night. Anyone who had left a light switch on could then find themselves an illuminated target in the middle of the blacked-out city. It was just another part of the game that was being played out with the innocent lives of the civilians trapped inside the city.

At its narrowest, the city is only 5 miles across, and at its widest 10. It was a miracle that anyone survived. If the Serbs had really wanted to raze the city to the ground, they could have, but I don't think that they wanted to occupy a ruin at the end of the conflict. They also wanted to gain the support of the outside world and could not understand why the West was not being more supportive in what they saw as the front line against the domination of Islam. What they did not understand was that it was the way they were going about it that was their downfall. Ethnic cleansing would never be an acceptable solution to the problem. Negotiations between the two sides continued to take place in our compound on a weekly basis, which in itself was a big step in the right direction. A really positive move was getting them to agree to hold pro-rata simultaneous prisoner exchanges which took place at the airport.

I had to photograph these exchanges from a hidden vantage point as neither side wanted the world to see what was going on, or how they had treated their prisoners. These exchanges were all about timing. On a prescribed day, at a given hour, the two convoys of prisoners would be escorted into the airport at exactly the same moment. The Serbs brought their prisoners in covered lorries and the Bosnian prisoners came in buses. Each convoy held exactly one hundred prisoners whose identities had to be checked by both sides before the exchange could be made. The prisoners would line up facing each other across our compound and only once both sides were satisfied could the exchange begin. You could see the anguish on the faces of the prisoners as they waited for the exchange to take place. Many had been in captivity since the very beginning of the siege and had obviously been mistreated. Some of the poor souls were in a bad way both physically and mentally, so weak that they could not walk the last few yards to freedom unassisted. Many looked bewildered, some were crying, the occasion too much for them to take in. When they had boarded the transport, I am sure that many of them thought that they were being taken away to be executed. Most just looked at the ground, incapable of looking into the eyes of those they passed as the exchange was finally made. It took a couple of hours to verify every identity before the convoys were eventually ready to leave. I have never experienced anything quite like it.

We had to escort the convoys back to their own lines to prevent either side from opening up on the other before reaching safety. It was ridiculous, but again it was all part of the game. The exchanges were repeated several times during our stay – we even managed to get some of the opposing negotiators to shake hands and even get on first-name terms. Although the press had got wind that the exchanges were taking place, we had no choice but to refuse them entry to the base. They were allowed in when the weekly negotiations were held but unless they were told that there would be someone important taking part, they wouldn't turn up.

Just before one such meeting a very strange incident took place in front of the world's press. As normal, our compound was the venue for the meeting and on this occasion every TV and news crew had been told that there would be some high-ranking officials at this particular meeting. Nothing happens by chance in this world. The arrival of General Philippe Morillon of France and General Ratco Mladic of Serbia at the entrance to the conference building was timed to perfection. Every camera was pointed at the pair and the flashlights were working overtime. This was one of those photo opportunities not to be missed and the photographs would appear on the front of every national newspaper in the world within hours. As the TV cameras rolled and the journalists shouted out to catch the attention of the pair, General Mladic turned to face the cameras and held his hand out to General Morillon. Morillon made a grand overt gesture of refusal and stormed into the building. Within hours the images would be beamed up to satellite links and be on every evening news bulletin.

Once both parties were inside the building and well out of sight of the press, they got down to a friendly game of table tennis as if they were old palls. With the meeting over, they again left at the same time. The TV cameras rolled and still cameras clicked hoping for more of the same, but this time they did not look at the press or each other before getting into their respective vehicles. It was all for the cameras. The pair of them would not have been out of place in Hollywood. Another example of how the public are manipulated for whatever reason.

As the winter weather worsened it became clear to us that large parts of the population were suffering more than others from a shortage of food and warm clothing. When the aid convoys arrived in the city they were taken to warehouses run by the different communities, depending on the source of the aid. If it came from a Christian charity, then it went to a warehouse run by the Christian community. The problem was that 70 per cent of all aid coming in was from Christian charities. The small percentage of aid coming in by air was given out to everyone regardless of which community they were from. I was shocked to find aid which had originated from Scottish Christian Aid charities was piled high in a warehouse. From the paperwork we could see that it had arrived months before and was not being distributed to non-Christian communities.

We visited a Roman Catholic church hall which was stacked to the roof with aid parcels. If you weren't a Catholic, you did not get one. It was that simple. We visited every Christian denomination in the city and found the same thing. It was so bad that our Colonel decided to initiate our own distribution system. We bullied, coerced or simply confiscated supplies from the mountains of aid lying in the warehouses. The problem had arisen because the Christian population was of Serbian nationality and hated the rest of the population, despite being shelled by their own people. You had a siege within a siege. But this was humanitarian aid sent to the people of Sarajevo, regardless of the background of the donors. The aid had not been sent with a proviso attached dictating who would receive it. The people at home who had given so generously would have been horrified if they had known the truth.

Our efforts had only a limited effect on the larger problem of feeding the population. We supervised and protected the distribution operations in the worst-affected areas. For several months we more or less commandeered the aid convoys as they came into the city. They had to pass by the airport anyway before they could enter the city, and despite their protests we forced them to distribute the aid direct to the areas where there was the most suffering. In some instances this was the first aid to reach them since the start of the siege.

I am afraid the truth is that only a small percentage, about 20 per cent, of all items handed in to charity shops, or collected by well-meaning organizations, ever finds its way to the people needing it most. Most of it ends up on the black market or pays for the administration costs of the so-called charities. I have watched as parents cut grass to make soup, such was their desperation. Every spare bit of ground in Sarajevo was planted with vegetables and potatoes. It was difficult to prevent our efforts to ensure that aid was distributed being exploited for political gain, or from being used against us in an attempt to destroy our neutrality.

One such incident in particular sticks in my mind and is worth commenting on. We received an invitation to attend a 'cultural event' in the Bosnian district of Dobrinja. Our Colonel and senior officers were asked to attend the event in the 'Community Centre' which had been a hall constructed for the 1984 Winter Olympics. The invitation was accepted on condition that we could search the venue and that it would be secured by our own men – there was an obvious security risk with so many senior personnel in the same place at the same time. We also let them know every Bosnian mortar battery would be put under observation to prevent a repeat of the 'market' incident. You can just see the headlines: 'Serbs bomb UN delegation on peacekeeping mission.'

The 'cultural event' turned out to be an art exhibition and concert given by the city's leading artists and musicians. The artwork and photography depicted the suffering of the city during the siege and was of the highest standard. This was followed by a two-hour concert by what was billed as the 'Bosnian National Orchestra'.

As we were shown to our seats at the front of the hall we could see that the members of the audience were all dressed as if they were at the Proms in the Royal Albert Hall in London. The ladies were wearing evening dresses and the men were in dinner suits. We of course were dressed in full combat gear, carrying assault rifles. When we got to our seats the curtains suddenly opened to reveal the orchestra, and ... a Bosnian TV film crew. It was evident that they intended to broadcast the event. Here was a sophisticated audience of cultured people in the presence of armed UN soldiers – a bit like Hitler in full uniform at the opera. The impression they would try to give was that we were obviously working with the Serbs to keep them imprisoned within their own city. The concert, like the art exhibition, was excellent but our Colonel was one step ahead of the game.

The CRAP were waiting as the film crew left the building by the back door, and the film was confiscated.

Manipulation is a new factor which must always be taken into account by peacekeeping forces in today's conflicts. Not only does it endanger the neutrality of the UN, but can put the lives of the peacekeepers at risk. The presence of 'on the spot' news crews complicates the work of the peacekeeping forces. It also requires the deployment of valuable personnel to protect them when they could be better deployed doing something else.

Whether the news crews agree or not, their safety is our responsibility and that is something that we take very seriously. It also affects your operational thinking when there is a camera filming your every move. There are times when a film crew will try and stage manage an incident just to get some footage to sell. Most of the film crews in war zones are freelance and sell their footage to the highest bidder. The reporter, or rather correspondent, then does a piece to camera in the safety of a hotel room and the editors back home put the two films together, even though the correspondent was nowhere near the incident in question.

It is amazing how the presence of a news team can turn an aggressor into a victim before your very eyes. As if by magic, injured babies and children appear out of the blue, complete with wailing mothers, even when there was no one about before the arrival of the camera crew. Suddenly a minor incident draws an angry crowd, forcing you to use force to protect the film crew, who in turn make it seem as if it was you who was the aggressor. You can be sure that by the time the edited footage gets onto your TV screen during the evening news, it will bear no resemblance to the actual incident.

I have witnessed TV crews paying children to throw stones at soldiers and tanks, knowing full well that they will eventually get a reaction from the soldiers. The resulting footage will only show the aggressive soldiers, not what caused them to react like that. If a child dies or is seriously injured, so much the better, it sells well to the networks.

Another incident highlighted the dangers we faced from this kind of manipulation. This time it happened at the Serbian checkpoint in Ilidza. A UN convoy which had driven up from the Adriatic pulled into the checkpoint. Normally the checks on UN vehicles were restricted to documentation and control of the vehicle contents. On this occasion the convoy was made up of five 20-ton flatbed trucks and their military escort. The lorries had platforms that tipped and rolled the loaded containers onto the ground while still loaded.

The Serbian controller insisted that the container on the second lorry be rolled off onto the ground to reveal the lorry chassis. This was something that had never been done before and why had they picked on this lorry? While the containers were being offloaded, several TV film crews suddenly appeared to record the proceedings. This they claimed was to show how honest and efficient the Serbian authorities were and that they had nothing to hide. The officer in charge of escorting the convoy had no objections and the container was quickly removed. While the flatbed of the lorry was still raised, the controller walked straight up to the chassis and – surprise, surprise – pulled out a metal ammunition case from within the framework. He shouted to the film crew and quickly pointed out several other similar cases hidden inside the chassis – ten cases in total on each side, filled with AK47 rifle ammunition. In front of the cameras, accusations were made that the UN were smuggling munitions into the city in contravention of everything and anything you could think of. A Serbian dignitary appeared within minutes and proceeded to read out a long speech which must have taken hours to write. The whole episode was a set-up with the cooperation of the world press, who didn't care if it was a set-up as long as it was a good story.

The strange thing was that they didn't examine any of the other lorries. Humanitarian aid ground to a halt for several days until it was pointed out that the lorry in question had been hired from a Serbian contractor two days before the convoy had set off from the coast. The vehicle had been sprayed white before delivery and some of the ammunition boxes had traces of white paint on them from the spray job, proving that they had been in place before the UN accepted the lorry from the contractor. I don't know why, but the press didn't get round to publishing that piece of information.

The saddest part was that no senior UN person stepped forward to defend the convoy personnel who had been removed from operational duties. They were reinstated later but without any public apology. It didn't matter to the hierarchy if some minions fell by the wayside – they would get a peerage or whatever honours their countries handed out when it was all over.

When I eventually left the Legion I should have perhaps taken more photographs with me but those I took in my official capacity as regimental photographer belong to the Legion and I have no moral or legal right to use them.

Any delay in aid coming into the city meant real hardship for its inhabitants and the arrival of an aid convoy was always a big event. Normally we were warned well in advance of their arrival but every now and again something would go wrong. All convoys arrived by the same route, even if it meant a hundred mile detour to get onto it.

On 6 March, everyone was taken by surprise when at exactly 10.00 am, eight unescorted civilian lorries came to a halt outside our gate at the northern entrance. It must have passed the Serbian barracks, but because no convoys ever came that way they had been able to drive right up to the barrier without passing through a checkpoint. Our men at the guard post could see that both sides were nervously taking up battle stations. They were as much in the dark about the situation as we were. To further complicate the situation, the lorries were all old, had Serbian number plates and did not look like an international aid convoy.

Our Colonel was not at the airport and the senior officer in charge would not make a decision about whether or not to let them pass into the airport. He paced about the ops room, unable or unwilling to take control of the situation. Our guard post was reporting ever-increasing activity and could see a Bosnian unit armed with RGP7 anti-tank rockets taking up position opposite the convoy. It was obvious that someone would open up on the vehicles at any minute but still our officer would not make his mind up.

The decision was taken out of his hands when the Bosnians fired three rockets at the lead lorry, killing its occupants. Immediately both sides opened up on each other, with the convoy stuck in the middle. The Bosnians obviously thought that this was a Serbian convoy trying to get into the city through the back door. The Serbs didn't know what the hell was going on but they were Serbian lorries and they were under attack.

At this moment our Colonel came on the air from his vehicle and ordered our men at the guard post to open fire on both sides with everything they had, to keep their heads down. He also ordered reinforcements to the area to back them up. He was only minutes from the airport and immediately he arrived in the ops room he got on the hotlines to arrange a ceasefire.

The leading vehicle of the convoy had burned out and the rest were badly shot up. As soon as the exchanges of fire began to ease off our Colonel ordered the NCO in charge of the guard post to get a UN flag onto a pole and lead a patrol out onto the road to bring any survivors into the base. We didn't know who they were or where they had come from but there were civilians out there needing our help. Six civilians lost their lives, four had serious wounds and, miraculously, six came out of it unscathed. We had no idea how many casualties there had been among the opposing factions. It turned out that the convoy was from a Serbian Christian organization trying to bring aid into the city. It took three days to drag the lorries into the airport and clear the road of debris. They had been carrying perishable goods which were now only fit for dumping.

It is impossible to convey to anyone who has not been in a war zone the effect incidents like this have on you when your nerves are already stretched to breaking point. Everyone is under enormous stress and incidents like this get blown up out of all proportions in your mind.

One evening I was asked to run the French Military Attaché to the Bosnian Army (he was not a Legion officer) from the airport into the city where he had accommodation. It was getting late, darkness was beginning to fall and I didn't much fancy running the risk of driving back to the airport after the UN roadblock had been withdrawn. On my way into town I made sure that the checkpoint commander knew that I was intending to come back as soon as I had dropped off my passenger and asked if he would delay his withdrawal to the airport for as long possible. It was up to him to make the decision and it would be a close call. I couldn't ask him to put himself and his men in danger – I could always spend the night at the UN HQ in the PTT building.

My little VBL was not exactly a sports car, but we made it to his quarters in the centre of the city on record time. I was on the move before my passenger even had time to say thank you or good night and headed off on the return journey. The city was closed down for the night and the habitual nightly shelling was just starting. The streets were totally deserted, there was no one, not even a dog and it was very eerie. By now the sky was getting pretty dark, there was heavy cloud cover and it looked like it might snow. As I flashed past the Holiday Inn, I got on the radio to the checkpoint to confirm that I was on my way, but couldn't raise them. Reception in this part of the city was not good but I could hear a broken transmission coming over the air and assumed that it was the checkpoint trying to reply to my call. As I passed the PTT building I saw that I was doing almost 80 mph in a vehicle designed to do 50.

At the point where I would turn off the main road for the airport, I had to pass the Bosnian checkpoint under the flyover. Fortunately for me, they had taken cover inside their shelter for the night and were probably hitting the bottle. There was no way that I was slowing down or going to stop and when I looked in my wing mirror I saw several Bosnian soldiers dashing out of the bunker into the road to see what it was that had roared past them at high speed. The UN checkpoint was by now only a couple of hundred yards down the road and I was very relieved to see that the VAB was still in place. They pulled back to let me through and fell in behind me as we made our way to the safety of the airport. Our departure was greeted by the rattle of gunfire from both sides of the road, but nothing hit us and I am sure that both sides were having a good laugh at our expense.

On my return to the command centre I thanked the checkpoint commander for waiting for me. Unknown to me calls had been made on the hotlines advising them of my late return. I was still not happy that our lives had been put at risk. The officer could easily have stayed at the airport overnight. I was so uptight about it that I was in danger of overstepping the mark so was taken aside by my boss who told me to go and calm down. He was right, of course, I was blowing the incident out of all proportion, but it was just another sign of the stress we were all under.

Our daily contact with the outside world was by a sat-link telephone which we were allowed to use for ten minutes once a week. There were no mobile phones or laptops in those days and they would have been banned anyway for security reasons. I am astonished to see soldiers on the front line these days using mobile phones, never mind phones with cameras. It is not that you shouldn't be able to keep in touch with your friends and family, it is just not professional or safe to have unsecure communications in a war zone. It's a security nightmare. With modern technology you can pinpoint the exact position of any mobile phone. Once that is done all you have to do is feed the coordinates into a guidance system on a missile, and bingo, you have a direct hit. It's crazy. Even if you are not using it but it is switched on, it can be tracked. This is not the stuff of fictional films, it exists now and can be bought by anyone over the Internet.

Our secure phone link was operated by a great bunch of lads from the Danish signals unit. They bent over backwards to provide us with this fragile link to our families. You had to pre-book the call and the clock would start as soon you started to speak. You were interrupted thirty seconds before the end of the call to give you a chance to say your goodbyes. It was like speaking into a tin can and you had to get used to the few seconds delay every time you spoke or you ended up talking over each other. The ten minutes flew past and at the end you found that you hadn't said half of what you meant to say. But it was still a great morale booster. We knew that the calls were listened in to and that we would be cut if we said anything that could be interpreted as confidential in a military sense.

There were times when you felt like revealing the truth about was really happening, especially when you were told what had been on the news back home. Some countries gave a far better factual coverage than others, and you felt like saying, 'That's nothing like what's happening here.' Some reporters were great to work with and were more interested in telling the true story than they were in making themselves out to be the story. There were also incidents that made it very hard to believe that what you were doing was right, or to have any faith in the honesty and motives of those who were supposedly trying to bring about peace.

CHAPTER 16

My Personal Shame

In 1993, the Ukranian battalion working with UN (UKRBAT), was assigned to keep the peace in the demilitarized Muslim enclaves of Zepa, as well as the Serbian district of Ilidza, where the Serbian military headquarters were. They seemed to be keeping the Bosnians prisoner in the Bosnian enclaves rather than keeping the Serbs out. This observation became a fact when we visited the Muslim enclave of Zepa. I have already recounted how they manipulated the system for financial gain, and were openly hostile to the Muslim population in Sarajevo. We were getting intelligence reports from a region on the southern frontier of Bosnia with Serbia, that entire villages were being burned to the ground and that the inhabitants were being herded like cattle into the mountains round the enclave of Zepa.

After pressure was applied on the UN authorities by our Colonel, it was reluctantly decided that the allegations would have to be investigated. 1st Company was given the task, and Captain D and myself were attached to them to gather and record evidence of any genocide. My problem was that I had to hide my photographic equipment to get it past the many checkpoints we knew we would encounter en route. I took the panel off the engine cover inside the VAB we were sharing with the CRAP, and wrapped my photographic equipment and video camera inside heat-resistant foil, before putting it inside the engine compartment. There was no access to this part of the engine from outside the vehicle so I was confident that the equipment would not be found.

Our route took us through Pale where the Serbs had set up their regional parliament. It was also the home town of Radovan Karadic, leader of the Serbian Democratic Party in Bosnia, who has at last been caught and will be facing charges before the International War Crimes Tribunal. Pale was, or had been, a prosperous market town which also profited from the 1984 Winter Olympics. How different it all was now. The civil war was not only tearing the country apart, but had plunged it into poverty that was affecting everyone. There will always be those who profit from situations like this – the criminal gangs, arms dealers, politicians and journalists.

We didn't stop in the town, but everywhere there were the signs that Pale played an important role in the Serbian war effort. We got glimpses of heavy armament, anti-aircraft weapons, tanks and all the other trappings you associate with a major military force. I couldn't risk taking any photographs in case I jeopardized the principal mission, and we were still a long way from our destination.

We were delayed at a couple of checkpoints, but on the whole we did not detect any particular delaying tactics out of the ordinary. We were quite a large force with twenty-one VABs, sixteen of which carried a full combat group, the other five being a command unit, a signals unit, an ambulance, our own VAB and a unit of the CRAP acting as our escort – 160 legionnaires are not a force to be messed about with.

As we got closer to the region in question, we began to see evidence of villages having been attacked. Every Muslim family had been forced out of their homes and if a Serb did not want the property, it was burned to the ground. We had no idea at this stage as to the whereabouts of the evicted families. No one we spoke to had seen or heard anything and all questions were answered with a shake of the head and a shrug of the shoulders. If the reports coming in were correct, they were all being shepherded towards Zepa. We had no idea just how many people we were talking about, but it was obvious from the number of burnt-out houses that we were talking about thousands rather than hundreds. Our final push into Zepa was quite tense. The Serbian troops gave way to large numbers of Ukrainian soldiers, and they were not happy to see us. There was a distinct lack of friendly waves or smiles as we passed through their lines – none of the usual friendly greetings normally exchanged between one UN force when it met up with another.

The countryside we had been passing through was typical of farming communities anywhere in the world. There were rolling fields and a few animals here and there. We were a lot further south and although well out of the mountains that surrounded Sarajevo, it was still cold at night. There were signs that spring was approaching but we were some way inland and still well above sea level. The mountains were replaced by hills scarred by deep gorges and fast-running rivers. The hillsides were covered with huge pine forests and if it had not been for the circumstances we found ourselves in, it would have been a pleasure to be there.

The other strange thing was that this area had been declared a UN safe haven. Even after we had passed through the Ukrainian lines, we came across S0erbian soldiers dug in facing into the zone. This could only mean that the Serbs were free to come and go as they pleased which was in contravention of UN Resolutions.

As we descended into the gorge cut out of the hillside by the River Drina, it was like descending into another world. It was quite beautiful but there was no sign of any human life until we broke out of the tree line near the bottom of the ravine. With its steep-sided gorge and fast-flowing river we could have been back in Corsica. The road crossed the river beside a watermill, before following the river towards the town. Our first sight of Zepa was of the minaret of the Islamic Mosque towering above the small stone cottages. We stopped in the middle of the village, which appeared to be deserted, but I could see that we were being watched from behind drawn curtains.

Captain D and I got out and decided to replace our helmets with our berets. It was less aggressive looking and we were going to have to gain the confidence of anyone who came out to speak to us. We had brought one of our female interpreters with us, but for the moment she stayed inside the safety of the VAB. We had no idea what their response to us turning up in the middle of the village was going to be.

A good twenty minutes passed before an elderly man tentatively approached us. He didn't speak any English or French so we called on our interpreter to join us. He said that we were the first outsiders they had seen, other than the Ukrainians, since the start of the war. We explained who we were and that we had come to investigate the rumours of ethnic cleansing. That made him laugh and he shouted out that it was OK for others to join us.

They claimed that the Ukrainians had come into the village a couple of months earlier and had beaten some of the younger inhabitants who they claimed were Islamic terrorists. They had threatened to hand everyone over to the Serbs if they didn't do what they were told. A large number of people had been herded into the region and their numbers had risen to such an extent that the village could not accommodate them. A combination of the overcrowding, shortage of food and the beatings had forced all but the most infirm and elderly to flee into the hills and onto a high plateau to the south of the village. The only access to the area was by a steep and narrow forest track which was just wide enough for a VAB to be driven along.

One of the village elders eventually agreed to go into the hills to make the initial contact while we waited overnight in the village for his return. 1st Company's VABs were loaded with basic food aid packages and these were offloaded into the Mosque. We explained that it was up to the village elders to distribute what we had brought but it was evident that it was not anywhere near to what was needed, never mind the thousands they said were up in the hills.

In the morning, Captain D, the interpreter and I left the Company in the village and drove up into the forest until we came to a large clearing where trees had been felled to form a barrier. The elder with us explained that we would have to go the last half mile on foot. The three of us had to carry my photographic and video equipment up the hillside until we came out onto a plateau which had been left by old logging operations. The elder asked us to wait five minutes while he went to collect the group who were going to talk to us. We would have to convince them that we were genuinely there to help them – no one else had so why should they believe us?

Half an hour later he returned with two gaunt-looking men armed with AK47 assault rifles. We had made a small campfire and had brewed some fresh coffee. We had taken off our flak jackets but had left our weapons within easy reach should things go badly. Captain D was gambling that our gestures would help to ease the fears of the men now approaching us.

After an hour's dialogue we persuaded them to take us into the forest to see how they were living. They also agreed that I could take photographs and video their living conditions to show the world how they were being treated by the Serbs, with the help of the Ukrainians. What I saw shocked me. I can claim to have seen a bit of life in my time, but nothing prepared me for this. Hundreds, perhaps thousands, of human beings were living in conditions that man has not experienced since cavemen inhabited the planet. There were very few adult males in the community – they had been executed by the Serbians when they burned down their homes.

They were living in shelters made out of branches covered with leaves, in exactly the same way I had seen pygmies in Africa build their shelters – the difference was that the pygmies were good at it. The other difference was that this was central Europe, not tropical Africa. Some had managed to find clothing, but the majority had resorted to making clothes out of animal skins. They were living off the forest, catching what little food they could find. Their diets were supplemented by fish caught in the river, but they explained that it was too dangerous to go down to the river when it was still daylight because Serbian snipers would fire on them from the other side of the ravine. This also meant that the Serbs were operating almost 10 miles inside the supposed 'UN safe haven'. Now we understood why they doubted why we were there.

They had no contact with the outside world other than what they gleaned from new arrivals in the forest. They knew nothing about the peace negotiations and put little faith in them anyway. These were poor village people who happened to be Muslim by birth, caught up in a war that they did not understand. One man had hauled an old treadle sewing machine up into the forest. Apart from making clothes he used it to power a generator which produced enough electricity to run an old transistor radio. The only radio station he could get was the BBC World Service but he didn't really understand what was being said, and he had only heard Bosnia mentioned a couple of times anyway.

They could see no end to their nightmare. They were desperately short of food and clothing and had no medical supplies whatsoever. It was then that Captain D decided to organize a relief air drop. The only suitable drop zone was an exposed plateau which was within range of Serbian artillery. There was no other choice. The drop would have to take place at night and although the DZ was small, it was hoped that enough of the supplies would land on the target to make it worthwhile. We returned to the VAB, made radio contact with UN headquarters in Sarajevo and it was arranged that the US would make a drop the following night. We returned to the group to tell them the news.

We would have to mark out the DZ with flares at the last moment but we would talk the aircraft onto the DZ. We spent the night in the forest to gain the confidence of the refugees. I suspect that if the drop had not gone ahead, we would never have made it out of there alive. They were not totally convinced that we were not there to spy on them for the Serbs, as the Ukrainians had been doing. I took lots of photographs of the women and their starving, emaciated children. It reminded me of the photographs I had seen of Jews in concentration camps in the 1940s, and this was our brave new world of 1993. I knew that this would be valuable evidence if anyone was ever brought to justice at a later date, although I should have known better. Because of my experience as a police photographer I knew exactly what kind of photographs to take.

The first pass was a bit of a disaster. It was no one's fault as there was a strong wind blowing at ground level and the DZ was so small. The pilots were reluctant to fly too low because they felt to do so would tell the Serbs what they were doing and they would open fire on the DZ. The drop from the first aircraft saw the packages fall into the ravine and most of the supplies were washed away. It was then decided to risk a lower pass and the second drop was spot on. They used a technique called the 'crush box' for the drops. This was more accurate than by parachute and the cardboard containers crushed and absorbed the shock of the impact against the ground. These initial drops were mostly American ration packs which come in the form of plastic sachets that were able to withstand being dropped from a height.

What happened next illustrates the depths of despair that can be reached when people are fighting for their families' survival. They had been so deprived of food that a frantic battle started over each individual ration pack. A woman who had just managed to gather up half a dozen of the small ration packs was stabbed to death by another woman for her meagre supply. This was not a criminal act, this was the animal instinct to survive taking over. Eventually calm was restored and we tried to convince them that the drops would continue each night for as long as required. There would be enough for everyone.

We spent another day with them and I promised before we left that I would tell the world about their plight. We then returned to Zepa to rejoin the Company, before retracing our steps back to Sarajevo. I made sure that all the film and equipment was back in its hiding place before we started out on the return journey. The air drops would not have gone undetected and we expected the Serbs to be obstructive. As we passed through the Ukrainian lines there was not as much as a smile on their faces. Our presence in the area was far from welcome and they were glad to see the back of us. There were dozens of refugees passing through their lines into the enclave and we witnessed one of the Ukrainians taking a gold chain from the neck of an old lady. It was the price she had to pay to get into the 'safe haven'.

When we reached the official Serbian lines we were delayed as expected. At the back of the checkpoint area was a large armoured Mercedes with the grey-haired figure of Radovan Karadic watching the search. There was no doubt that his presence at the checkpoint showed that he knew exactly what was going on in the Zepa enclave and that they were working under his direct orders.

I had more than enough photographic evidence of the atrocious conditions these people were being forced to live under and felt good that at least I might be able to contribute something to the relief of these poor people.

It took us two days to get back to Sarajevo. The final stretch between Pale and Sarajevo was under mortar attack by the Bosnians and we had to wait a couple of hours until it was safe enough to proceed. After Captain D wrote his report on our findings, we went to the PTT building to present them to the most senior staff of the UN in Sarajevo. This included some of the politicians who had been chairing the peace negotiations taking place at the airport. I was told to hand over the films which would be sent to the UN facility in Zagreb for developing. After showing them the video footage I was instructed to leave it with them for 'safekeeping'.

We were forbidden to discuss the mission or any of our findings with anyone, in particular with the press. They said that the material was so sensitive that it would have to be dealt with through the proper channels. As the weeks passed, the air drops continued, but nothing else was happening. When I asked to see the photos I was told that there had been a technical problem in the development of the films and that all of the images had been lost. When I asked for the return of the video footage I was told that the subject was now classified and that the video had been sent elsewhere for assessment. It was no longer our problem and we should drop the subject.

I could have kicked myself for being so naive and for not making a copy of the video. When our Colonel made an official complaint he was told that it had been decided at the 'highest level' in the UN and that it was not in the public interest for our 'allegations' to be made public at this time.

I feel that I personally let those people down and I am ashamed at not exposing what was happening at the time. My only excuse is that I was a mere Caporal Chef and could not disobey an order given to me from on high. I do not blame my officers, but I do blame the politicians who could not care less about anyone other than themselves. I recently heard the very same person who had been one of the chief UN negotiators in Bosnia, saying in a radio interview that economic sanctions were not the answer to Russia's invasion of Georgia. Of course, the fact that he was on the board of one of Russia's largest oil-exporting companies has absolutely nothing to do with it.

In hindsight my decision not to speak out was morally wrong. Two years later I heard the UN authorities say that they had no way of knowing about, or preventing, the Srebrenica region massacres. This area includes Zepa. At the time, I wrote a letter to my future wife explaining what I had just witnessed. Despite it being opened and heavily censored, she tells me that it was so full of anger that she could not keep it after reading it. The incident has troubled me ever since and it has been hard to write about it. The experience has made me think very hard about what we were being asked to do, and why we were doing it. There is no doubt in my mind that politicians are the most dangerous animals on the planet. They play games with the lives of the very people they were elected to serve, simply to satisfy their own agendas.

It is true that a soldier is there to serve and obey, to carry out lawful orders. Whether it be for King and Country or as part of a UN peacekeeping force, it is not the place of the soldier to question the motives behind the orders. But you shouldn't be put in that position in the first place. Sadly that does not stop you thinking about it, especially when you are the ones seeing first hand the results of these orders. Unfortunately the politicians are not the ones being put on the spot. If they are, they just resign, get knighted and use their name to move on to a lucrative position or directorship somewhere.

Everyone was tired and stressed out. Tempers were getting short and our Colonel saw that we all needed to have a bit of a break. It was not possible to give anyone leave outside the country, but there were regions of the old Yugoslavia that were more or less untouched by the war. Our Croatian NCO had members of his family who lived in the Croatian seaside resort of Primosten, only a few miles up the coast from Split, which itself was only half an hour away by plane from Sarajevo. The area was deemed safe enough for everyone to have a week's break. The local hotels were crying out for business and, using his family connections, our NCO struck a deal with a fairly modern hotel to take a different section every week. Everything was paid for by the Regiment, including the supply of a small selection of civilian clothes for us to wear. I am glad to say that military uniforms were not allowed.

My turn didn't come until the last group, and that was almost at the end of our fifth month in Sarajevo. The only advantage was that it was now the end of May and the weather was a good 10 to 15 degrees warmer than it was in Sarajevo. The worst of the cold weather had passed and it would be nice to feel the warmth of the sun on our faces.

We flew into the civilian airport at Split and changed out of our military uniforms in the toilets. It was only a short bus trip down the coast to Primosten and it was hard to believe that less than an hour earlier we had been in the middle of a war in the same country. I could see why the Adriatic coast had become a favourite holiday resort with the British before this conflict started. The beaches were deserted but it was great to see the sea.

The hotel was typical of the 1960s/1970s concrete buildings which had been constructed during communist rule. Everything was a bit basic but spotlessly clean. Primosten itself is a lovely little town with a small marina, a couple of good restaurants, bars and some small gift shops. There were no tourists as such, although there were one or two private yachts from an Italian sailing club which were berthed in the marina.

The locals were very welcoming and overall the atmosphere was just what the doctor ordered. Most of our time was spent relaxing in the harbour bars just watching the world go by. I had brought a sketch book and some watercolour paints with me, and was content to just sit on the quayside and paint. I even went to the local barber and had a haircut.

Unfortunately, by the time we had started to relax, it was time to head back to Sarajevo – something that none of us were looking forward to. We enjoyed a good meal together in the hotel on the last night, but the stress was coming back and the conversation was stilted. We were all preoccupied with what the next month would hold for us.

We all withdrew into ourselves and, on reflection, I wonder if psychologically it was a good idea to give us this break. Over the past five months we had built up our own way of dealing with the stress. This break had lowered our defences and made it harder for us all to cope with the last stint in Sarajevo. At Split airport it was back into combat gear and flak jackets for the flight back to Sarajevo. You could have heard a pin drop. As soon as the aircraft dropped its nose for the descent into the airport, the lads seemed to switch into soldier mode. Heads came up and everyone was alert and ready to go. The holiday was now a thing of the past and it was business as usual.

One thing had changed. There had been a huge reduction in the numbers trying to cross the airport at night. There were several contributing factors: the amount of humanitarian aid actually finding its way to those who needed it most, and the nightly bombardment of the city had eased quite a bit. I think that the Serbs were finding it harder to obtain a regular supply of ammunition, but the most important factor was without a doubt the tunnel.

We had no interest in finding it officially. If we had, some bright politically correct politician would have had us close it down. As long as it wasn't a threat to the security of the airport, and was helping to reduce the casualty figures of both those trying to cross and of our own men, we were content to let it be. What was disturbing were the rumours of how the access to the tunnel was being controlled. We were told that it was in the hands of the warlords who also just happened to be members of the local Mafia. If you couldn't pay, you couldn't use it.

We suffered a couple of serious injuries during our last couple of weeks at the airport. One lad was shot in the head and the other received two gunshot wounds in his left leg. The Legionnaire with the head injury received a full pension after a considerable period of rehabilitation. But fortunately our time in Sarajevo had come to an end and it was time for us to hand over operations to our replacements. Another Legion regiment in the form of the 2nd Infantry Regiment from Nimes was replacing us and their Colonel in Chief had been an old boss of mine in the BOI in Calvi back in the early 1980s.

We had been instructed to hand over all the information we had gathered during the past six months to the incoming detachment, but there was one major problem. I had more or less been given a free hand to perform my task as I saw fit and had created a role that had not existed before. That was the problem, because they didn't have anyone nominated to take over from me. The two colonels, who had worked together in the REP, got their heads together and agreed that I should stay on with the 2nd REI for an indefinite period – but only if I agreed. It took me all of five seconds to decide. I was flattered to be thought of so highly, but no! I had had enough and I was going home to Calvi as planned. As if by magic someone was found to replace me and I spent the next couple of weeks bringing him up to speed. A young Lieutenant was given the task and I think that he was looking forward to doing something a little bit different. At least I had done a lot of the groundwork and he only had to continue along the same lines.

Our greatest satisfaction was that we felt that the airport and its surroundings were a much safer place than they had been when we had taken over six months before. Was it really only six months? It seemed as if we had been there for years.

When the main detachment of the 2nd REI arrived, they were not given the same reception by the warring factions that we had received. To our surprise we were seen off by a delegation from both sides who thanked us for our unbiased efforts during our stay. Perhaps it had been worthwhile after all, but I don't think that the family of Legionnaire Benco would agree.

We walked to the aircraft carrying out flak jackets and wearing our green Legion berets, the blue UN ones already consigned to our pockets as souvenirs. As the aircraft left the runway a huge cheer broke out spontaneously. It was simply an explosion of nervous tension and there were quite a few wet eyes amongst us as the sudden realization struck home that we were finally on our way home safely and out of danger.

The flak jackets were passed to the back of the aircraft ready to be handed out to any new arrivals. When we landed at Zagreb we had time for a quick bit of duty free shopping in the terminal. The shops did a roaring trade in expensive watches for the lads and jewellery for wives and girlfriends.

The short flight back to Corsica was on an Air France 747. Because of the size of the aircraft and the weight of the freight it was carrying, the plane had to land in Bastia. This meant that we had to be bused back to Calvi – a delay of a couple of hours that we could well have done without. I think that if the flight had been diverted for a security search as before, there would have been a riot. Our Colonel flew back to the camp by helicopter.

It was a beautiful sunny afternoon when we eventually pulled up outside the camp. We could see that the main road outside the camp was lined by families, girlfriends and locals who had all turned out to welcome us home. The buses stopped short of the main gate and in true Legion tradition we formed up into our companies to march into the camp singing the Regimental song. The Colonel plus the officers and legionnaires who had remained in Calvi during our deployment formed a guard of honour. It was a moving moment for everyone and it was not just the families and friends who were fighting back the tears. I have never heard the Regimental song sung so well and with such pride. We were home.

In record time all our gear was put into storage for the night then we were released into the welcoming arms of our families and friends. The local bars, restaurants and night clubs had their busiest night of the season. My personal reunion would have to wait for a few days yet until I went on leave. Meanwhile, it was back to work first thing in the morning for all of us. Equipment had to be cleaned, sent for repair if required, then put back in storage ready for the next mission.

Exactly a week after our return, we departed on a well-earned month's leave. I headed for Scotland to be reunited with my family and partner. It was strange to walk the streets of Aberdeen, a city of comparable size to

Sarajevo, completely free of the stress and constraints of the past six months. There was no need to cower behind walls or be scared to cross a junction in case you got shot. I looked at the faces of everyone around me, going about the daily lives, oblivious to the horrors taking place just a couple of hours' flying time away.

It was impossible not to compare life here to that of Sarajevo; in fact, it made me realize that we do not connect with the misery of the masses in any war-torn country. What we watch on the news may horrify us for all of thirty seconds until it is time for the next episode of *Coronation Street* or *Eastenders*, but that's it. If you have not experienced the horror of war first hand, you can have no comprehension of what it is like to be caught up in one. No amount of coverage in the press or on TV can do that.

My wife to be and I enjoyed a couple of weeks in Scotland visiting our parents before heading back to Calvi by car. We spent another two weeks just meandering southwards through France in the general direction of Nice before catching the ferry back to Corsica. I was glad to be back on the island and looked on Calvi as my home.

Back at work I soon settled into the daily routine of life in the REP. Like everyone else, I was unaware of the amount of stress we had all been under. I felt good but it was only those around us who could see the changes. For me the biggest change was in the colour of my hair – it had gone from fair to almost pure white.

A couple of months after our return, it was announced that, apart from the UN Medal for Service to Peace in Bosnia awarded to everyone, some of us were to receive additional honours. To my surprise I was to be amongst those to be decorated. Like everyone else, I felt that I had done no more than was expected of me and in fact felt that I could have done more.

A medal ceremony was held in private with only the Regiment present. I, along with nine others, were presented with *La Croix de la Valeur Militaire avec Etoile de Bronze* (French Military Cross with Bronze Star) at Brigade level. The citation reads:

> While serving within the French Battalion in Sarajevo as part of the United Nations Protection Force since the 13th January 1993, in the course of a mission at the airport, came under fire from a sniper. Despite this, he continued the mission with calm determination.
>
> On the 23rd March 1993, while in the Battalion Command Post, was injured when fired on by an automatic weapon. His attitude while under fire warrants being cited.

I was also awarded a medal for being injured while on active service.

I am obviously proud to have been honoured in this way but every Legionnaire who risked his life while performing 'crossing' duties every night deserved it more than I did.

A few weeks later, the Minister of Defence, Francois Leotard, visited the Regiment and made a speech on behalf of the President of the Republic, thanking the Regiment, on behalf of the nation, for its contribution and human sacrifice, in the name of the peace process in Bosnia. He presented the Regiment with its eighth *Legion d'honneur*.

Several other honours were presented during the course of the ceremony, every one merited. The bravest and most moving sight of all was seeing Legionnaire Novokouski standing to attention, in full dress uniform and on his crutches, throughout the ceremony. This despite having lost his leg just six months before during the attack on the ambulance at the airport in Sarajevo. He refused to use the seat which had been provided for him. In honour of his personal sacrifice and courage, he was given French citizenship, a post at the French Military Headquarters in Paris and his family were brought from Poland to live with him in a flat provided by the Army. I wonder what would have happened to him if he had been in the British Army.

CHAPTER 17

Life Continues

Life goes on and I was soon off to complete my 17th and final GR20. There is nothing like the purity of the Corsican mountains to make you realize that it is man who creates all his own problems on this planet.

At the beginning of January 1994, the French government was looking at ways of reducing costs within the military. This led to them offering a financial package to anyone with more than ten, but less than fifteen years military service. They offered to pay a generous tax-free, one-off premium to anyone who wished to leave before they qualified for a full military pension, and the offer was extended to anyone in the Legion. I felt that as I was approaching fifty, it was getting harder for me to keep up the standard of fitness expected within the REP. Although I was still very fit, I did not want to keep going to the point where I could not keep up with the eighteen year olds. The incentive on offer was so attractive that I decided to accept it. The money would help me to set up in business in Calvi where I had been thinking about opening an art gallery.

My existing contract was up at the end of June 1994, so when the time came I headed off to Aubagne where my adventure had first started. I felt like I was leaving something that was more than just a job – it was like leaving my family behind for good. I had very mixed feelings about retiring and despite being offered a posting to the Legion magazine, *Le Kepi Blanc*, I had made up my mind. I was looking forward to my new life with my partner, who I knew was more than pleased that I would no longer be heading off on some dangerous destination. She would not have stopped me if I had decided to stay, but I had turned the page and I was ready for my next adventure.

We had rented a shop before I left for Aubagne and I still had my beautiful flat overlooking the port. I could visit the Regiment any time I wished and still had lots of friends in it. As already mentioned the old hospital in the Citadel was partly used by various clubs. One of these was a painting club for the wives and partners of legionnaires which was also open to the families of the Gendarmerie. I was asked to take over the club which met every Friday and was paid a retainer by the Regiment to teach at the club.

The Legion is a family like no other and this was illustrated the following year under very tragic circumstances. My American friend Joe, who had been the other victim of the shooting incident in the office in Sarajevo, fell ill. Joe was only in his late thirties and worked as a secretary in the Colonel in Chief's office. The Regiment was taking part in the Bastille parade on 14 July 1995 in Paris when Joe began to feel unwell. He couldn't keep his food down and a month later was diagnosed with advanced liver cancer. His health went downhill very quickly, requiring him to be transferred to the top military hospital in Paris. Our Colonel in Sarajevo who had left the Regiment, had just been promoted to the rank of a two-star General and was now based at the French Military Headquarters in Paris. When he heard about Joe's illness, he immediately arranged for Joe's mother to be flown from California to Paris to be at his bedside. The expense was covered by the Legion and I was asked to go to Paris by the Regiment to help his family at this difficult time.

It was clear that Joe was not going to survive more than a couple of months and the family were asked if they would like to take him home for the last few weeks of his life. He was flown to the States on a French military flight, accompanied by a male nurse who used to be in the REP. Joe knew him, which was a great help during the difficult journey. The flight was destined for Tahiti but was diverted into Los Angeles which was the nearest airport to Joe's family home.

When Joe died three weeks later, I flew to California for the funeral, accompanied by a Caporal who had worked with him in the office at Calvi. All our expenses were paid by the Regiment and the French Military Attaché to the US flew from Washington to represent the French Army officially. It was a moving experience and a further example of what it meant to be a part of the Legion family.

I know of no other military organization that shows this kind of loyalty and respect for its men, regardless of rank. A few years later General Poulet, our former Colonel, died suddenly of cancer while still a young man. His funeral was attended by active and ex-legionnaires of all ranks, who showed him the same respect and affection he had shown to his men. When you have served in the ranks of the Legion you are a Legionnaire before everything else, regardless of rank.

It is always difficult to adapt to the civilian way of life after years of military service. You miss the discipline and organization which seem to be missing in civvy street. Many find it impossible and fall on hard times. The Legion never turns its back on a comrade under such circumstances. They are taken into the safety of the Legion retirement home at Puyloubier in the south of France near Aubagne, where they are kept for as long as it takes to get them back on their feet. Some never leave.

Puyloubier is a small farm with residential accommodation. It produces red wine on a commercial basis in its vineyards and the residents manufacture Legion souvenirs which are sold in every camp shop and in the Legion Museum in Aubagne. The money raised goes towards the upkeep of the facility. A visit to the museum at Aubagne is well worthwhile.

I spent another seven happy years in Calvi running our art gallery before we returned to Scotland to help look after our elderly parents. I still look on Calvi as my home. I made many Corsican friends during my eighteen years on the island.

Like all professional soldiers, many legionnaires find it hard to get a job in civilian life which can provide the job satisfaction or excitement that they are used to. The qualifications and job skills you pick up in the military tend not to be on the list of qualifications being sought by civilian companies. Because of this, many find themselves seeking employment with the so-called security companies that have sprung up in recent years. Most offer jobs protecting commercial companies working on contracts in areas of armed conflict such as Iraq and Afghanistan.

When I joined the Legion in 1983, five of us trained together, joined the same regiment, served together over the years and have remained lifelong friends. Our little group was a mini United Nations on its own, being made up of a South African, a Canadian, a Japanese, a Vietnamese and myself. We did everything together and are, or rather were, like brothers. I use the word 'were' because one of them was killed doing what he did best – protecting the lives of others while risking his own. Akihito Saito was killed in Iraq in May 2005. Aki was part of a security team protecting a civilian group of workers near Hir, just west of Baghdad. The convoy was ambushed and a fierce battle erupted between the attackers and those guarding the convoy. Many in the convoy were killed during the initial attack but Aki fought on despite being severely injured. Before reinforcements arrived he was captured by a group of terrorists called Ansar al-Sunnah. They posted details of his capture on their website, but despite efforts by the Japanese authorities to negotiate his release, his body was found by the roadside on 28 May 2005, nineteen days after he was captured. Knowing Aki, he would have fought to the end to save those under his care without a thought for himself. He was employed by one of the better UK private security companies and was only forty-four.

Of the four of us remaining, the South African works in the security industry, the Vietnamese is a senior nurse in a military hospital in Paris and the Canadian has spent some of his time commercial diving in the Far East.

There comes a time in everyone's life, even the most adventurous of us, when you have to accept that it is time to move on and leave all the physical stuff to the young guys. There are always other ways of using your expertise.

CHAPTER 18

A Little Bit of History

I cannot finish my story without including a brief history of the operational activities of the 2ème REP. The first Legion parachute battalions were formed in Algeria in 1948 immediately after the Second World War – the 1st, 2nd and 3rd Parachute Battalions.

In Indochina (Vietnam), on the evening of 6 May 1954, after the battle of Dien Bien Phu, from the sixteen Legion battalions engaged in the action, 9,714 men were dead and 10,201 taken prisoner. This included the three parachute battalions and effectively led to them being disbanded.

On 1 September 1955, in Algeria, the 1st Parachute Regiment was formed, to be known as the 1er Regiment Etranger de Parachutists, or 1er REP. The 2eme REP was formed in December the same year.

The biggest changes in the history of the Legion took place in 1962. After almost ten years of civil unrest in Algeria, General de Gaulle told the people of Algeria that they were as much a part of France as was Brittany, and that France would never abandon them. Four days after his famous speech he gave the order for the total withdrawal of all French forces and administrative authorities from Algeria with immediate effect. This included the Legion who considered Algeria to be their home.

This did not go down well with the French military forces in Algeria, and in particular the Legion, who felt that they had shed their blood over the years for nothing. This gave rise to the famous 'Night of the Generals', when the five top French generals in Algeria led an open revolt by the Armed Forces. Plans were even made for the Legion Parachute Regiments to jump into Paris as part of a military coup. A compromise was reached at the last minute as a result of which the Legion was reduced in strength from 200,000 men to 10,000, and all of the regiments were dispersed throughout the French dominions: French Guyana in South America, Tahiti, Djibouti, Mayotte and Corsica. The headquarters were moved to Aubagne near Marseille in southern France.

The officer structure was reorganized and from that time no foreign officer could command a regiment, thus ensuring that control of what France still considered to be its best fighting units, stayed firmly under the control of Paris. The Paras were reduced to one regiment, the 2ème REP. The Regiment moved to its present base in Calvi on 17 December 1963. I can't say that I was aware of the upheaval in France at the time, but in those days news wasn't beamed into our living rooms in the same way it is today.

DJIBOUTI, 1976

We all think that Islamic terrorism is something new, and that what we are experiencing today is the fault of our leaders in the Western world interfering in the Middle East. That may help to aggravate the situation, but it is not the cause.

On 4 February 1976, the first terrorist attack by a Fundamental Islamist group called the Somali Coast Liberation Front (FLCS), took place in Djibouti. Thirty-one foreign children (mostly French) on board a school bus were taken hostage and driven to the frontier with Somalia, where their passage was blocked by the border guards. In exchange for the lives of the children, the terrorists demanded that all foreign forces and businesses leave the country, and that all political prisoners be set free. They also demanded that Djibouti should be declared a Fundamental Islamic Republic.

When the Republic of Djibouti gained its independence from France it maintained a military agreement with France to support and train its army. France also kept the right to have its own military bases within the Republic, which was home to the 14eme Demi-Brigade of the French Foreign Legion (14ème DBLE). 2nd Company of the REP was in the country on a four-month deployment when the hijacking took place. They were immediately sent to assist the local troops and a specialist unit of the Gendarmerie who had been flown out from Paris.

On the second day of the incident the situation began to deteriorate and it was decided that an intervention would have to take place before the children came to any harm. The order for the attack on the bus was given and the snipers from the Regiment simultaneously shot dead the hijackers without injury or loss of life to the children. Unfortunately one child was shot dead by a gunman from the Somalian side of the border.

This was a long time ago but nothing has changed. Nobody, it seems, saw the red lights flashing. I don't even think that the incident got more than a passing mention in the UK.

KOLWEZI, ZAIRE, 1978

Two years later in Zaire (now the Democratic Republic of the Congo), on 17 May 1978, the town of Kolwezi fell into the rebel hands of a group led by a

Major Mufi. The city of Kolwezi is on the Benguela Railway which links it to the port of Lobito in Angola. Kolwezi was a centre for a major copper and cobalt mining operation. Uranium, oxide ores and lime deposits were also plentiful. In the city were plants for processing the ores which were then shipped by rail to Likasi to the east, for exporting. Kolwezi was also the trade centre for the surrounding agricultural area.

Shaba Province, under the influence of Katanga, had attempted to break away from the newly independent Congo, which was formed in 1960. The breakaway movement had been defeated, but relations between the province and the central government remained poor. Sporadic fighting continued until 1978 when the province was invaded by separatist rebels who took over the city. Kolwezi was inhabited by over 3,000 Europeans, mainly mining experts and their families.

Zairian parachutists jumped into the city on 16 May but were quickly defeated. The Zairian leader, President Mobutu, asked for international assistance from the American, Belgian and French authorities which formed the majority of the foreign nationals trapped inside the city. The REP were alerted at their base in Calvi and, under the command of Colonel Philippe Erulin, the first elements of 1st, 2nd and 3rd Companies, plus part of HQ Company, took off in five DC-8 aircraft on the night of 17 May. The 4th and Support Companies flew out the following day.

Once in Kinshasa, the legionnaires were equipped with American parachutes borrowed from the Zairian Army, before leaving the following morning in four Hercules C-130s and one Transall, in very hot and cramped conditions for the four-hour flight to Kolwezi. Their arrival caught the rebels off guard and when they jumped on the outskirts of the city they met little initial resistance.

Although the REP were greatly outnumbered, nothing could halt the ruthless momentum of their attack. As the legionnaires started to clear large areas of the city, the Europeans began to emerge from cover, most of them hungry, thirsty and suffering from shock. Tragically, those being held in the Impala Hotel were killed before the legionnaires could reach them.

Within two hours the REP were almost in complete control of the city. A second wave of aircraft carrying the 4th and Support Companies, plus the remainder of HQ Company, were ordered to fly on to Lubumbashi to avoid a night drop. On the ground, the legionnaires continued to patrol and engage the enemy, killing many rebels. Unfortunately this success came at a price and the Regiment suffered half a dozen casualties.

The second wave jumped in during the early hours of the 20th but there was little fighting until the 4th Company ran into heavy resistance near Metal

Shaba, a district on the outside of the city. The rebels mounted an attack but were beaten off by Support Company's 81mm mortars and 89mm anti-tank rockets. The rebels fled leaving more than eighty bodies behind.

This was the last major action in Kolwezi and the Paras conducted a mopping-up operation. This operation confirmed the status of the REP as an elite force, but the Regiment went home with five dead and fifteen injured. It was later discovered that there were Belgian soldiers at an air base less than 20 miles from Kolwezi, and the Americans were still planning for the operation.

BEIRUT, AUGUST 1982

In August 1982, the REP were sent to the Lebanon and, in particular, Beirut. By 11.30 pm on the 20th, the Regiment had secured the harbour area and established a bridgehead for the arrival of the main UN force.

On the 26th they were given the mission of escorting Yasser Arafat and 4,371 Palestinian soldiers out of the region, which was a major contributory factor to peace being restored in the region.

The Regiment has been involved in many front-line peacekeeping operations, some of which I have covered in this book. Since my departure from the Legion in 1994, nothing has changed. The Regiment has been involved almost non-stop in peacekeeping missions throughout the world, except of course in the 2nd Gulf War where France refused to become involved.

I am more concerned about the innocent victims of today's conflicts than I am about the politics of the power seekers, but I am confident that Le Deuxième Regiment Etranger de Parachutistes, my Regiment, will continue to help those who are caught up in world conflicts which are not of their own making. It is important that we continue the fight against those who strive to destroy our way of life and the things we believe in.

My story is a real one. I have tried to relate it honestly without glorifying what I have experienced. Others no doubt will have had different experiences in the Legion and their points of view may differ. Of course there are things that happen and ways of doing things within the Legion that are a bit different from what you might experience in some other armies, but that is why it is the Legion. It's not the Boy Scouts and life can be tough at times, no one ever said it wouldn't be.

Most of the horror stories about the Legion that make their way into print are told by those who either never tried to join, did not pass selection, failed instruction or could not hack it for one reason or another and deserted. Many of these tales are told to justify their own actions or make themselves out to be something they aren't and never will be.

It was an honour and a privilege to have served in the French Foreign Legion and to have worked for, and with, some great guys.

I have tried to show that the Legion is made up of exceptional young (and not so young) men who, in many cases, have not only turned their own lives round, but have continued to show others by their example, bravery and determination that no one is ever too old to make a contribution towards making our planet a better and more peaceful place to live in. The life of a Legionnaire is not for everyone, or indeed within the grasp of everyone. I hope that having read my story you will appreciate that today's Legion plays an important part in the safety of today's world.

CHAPTER 19

Conclusion

Being a Legionnaire is nothing like you would expect. None of the thoughts you might have about it will come anywhere near the mark. The Legion has always had a reputation for being brutal and full of hard men and criminals. There is no doubt that it offers a hard physical world in which you are confronted with the realities of life at the sharp end. But then that is what being a soldier is all about. It does not matter if you are in the British Army, US Marines or the French Foreign Legion, if you only learn how to be physically dominant but know nothing about what it is like to be on the receiving end, the shock, when it happens to you, is likely to stress you out and cause you to crack up mentally.

We hear a lot these days about Post Traumatic Stress Disorder. So many soldiers are coming back home from war zones like Iraq and Afghanistan with PTSD that we need to be asking the question, why? It comes as no surprise to me that the percentage of legionnaires suffering from PTSD having been to those countries seems to be far lower than in the UK and US forces.

The Legion has been and still is engaged in all of the world's hot spots. From Africa to the Gulf, the Balkans and Afghanistan, the Legion has been on the front line as much as, if not more than, most of the countries involved in today's conflicts.

My story is not a recruitment drive for the Legion. If anyone reading this thinks that life in the Legion might be for them, there is nothing that I or anyone else can say, for or against, to help them decide. They will never know until they try it for themselves.

I keep reading on web forums about wannabe legionnaires who are going to join in six months' time, or next year, or whenever. Do you know something? They never will. The only thing that all future, serving and ex-legionnaires have in common is that they are all men of action. They don't talk about what they might or might not do at some future date, they just do it.

'Legio Patra Nostra'.